What others say about the book ...

"So often in my practice I am faced with distraught teachers who have been told something in secret and don't know what to promise the child; or who to tell when the parents don't respond; or even what the legal impact will be on themselves. Then there are the worried mothers who know it can happen because it happened to them, but have no practical information with which to tell if they are being paranoid or complicit. Most sad of all are the children themselves – who I invariably meet through a peer they have told, so often stuck in a situation where they don't want to lose their family, unsure whether it is something they are doing that is making it happen, and without the life experience to know what else to do to make it stop.

Plain speaking, and without pretensions, Bruna's writing has the immediacy of first-hand experience. It says that there is something horrible happening under our noses, far more often than we allow ourselves to believe. It tells you what to look for, how to avoid putting your own children at risk, and what steps to take to stop it if it's already happening.

In a world where nursery-school children can have porn videos sent to them on their cell phones; teenagers can send explicit images of themselves or their friends around the school in a matter of hours; and MXit and Facebook can provide predators with the perfect front to engage with uninformed teenagers, there is an urgent need for easily readable information to reach parents, teachers and teenagers.

This book is it!"

Sharon Doubell, Clinical Psychologist, Upward Spiral Psychology Consulting, Gauteng

* * *

"*Every Parent's Nightmare* is very informative and easy to read. The personal touch makes the reading easier and drives home the importance of the topic.

I recommend that anyone involved in the care of a child should read this book. The more informed we are, the better the chances of preventing the abuse.

This should be readily available reading in all schools and other venues where people may need to know about child abuse, both with regard to recognition and actions that should be taken.

I commend Bruna on this excellent contribution to the ongoing struggle against child abuse."

David Stanton, Course Co-ordinator Netcare 911 School of Emergency and Critical Care

* * *

"After reading this book I can honestly say that it mirrors the no-nonsense and easy to understand lectures that Bruna gives on the subject ... I think it is essential in arming those faced with these realities to better understand the subject.

I found the book both moving and informative; written passionately where necessary and dispassionately when appropriate. It presents the facts and informs the reader without invoking unnecessary emotion that so often messes up the process of dealing with abuse."

Darren van Zyl, Co-founder of the Medicare Academy of Emergency Care Training and AEA co-ordinator of COJEMS Training Academy, Johannesburg

* * *

EVERY PARENT'S NIGHTMARE

A practical guide for
dealing with

CHILD ABUSE

(2ND EDITION)

BRUNA DESSENA

Quickfox Publishing

Published by Quickfox Publishing
PO Box 50660 West Beach 7449
Cape Town, South Africa
www.quickfox.co.za
info@quickfox.co.za

First edition 2010
Second edition 2017

EVERY PARENT'S NIGHTMARE:
A Practical Guide for Dealing with Child Abuse
2nd edition: ISBN 978-0-620-77685-1

www.every-parents-nightmare.com

Editors – Daphne Stokoe & Rachel Bey-Miller
Cover and book designer – Vanessa Wilson
Typesetting and production – Quickfox Publishing
Printing – Digital Action SA, Cape Town, South Africa

Available from:
www.publisher.co.za, www.amazon.com, bookstores

Also available as an ebook

"If I have seen further than others, it is by standing upon the shoulders of giants."

Sir Isaac Newton

*"A trauma not transformed is
a trauma transferred."*

Ashley Judd, TED Talks

Dedication

If you have ever seen a child testify in a court of law then you will agree it is the most humbling experience.

As adults going to court we become nervous, even when we are not the defendant. Imagine what it is like for a child. These little people are not only expected to testify like an adult, they are expected to regurgitate facts, times, places, and accurately describe events when they don't even think in consecutive time as an adult does.

As adults, we struggle with the issue of a loved one leaving us, a lover who betrays us; imagine how children struggle with "I love my father, but I do not love what he does to me." They find it incredibly difficult to separate the person from the deed.

Every day there are men and women who help these little people with the unenviable task of testifying. This world is a better place since these giants are in it.

I dedicate this book to all the giants who have enriched my life –

- Agnes Bezuidenhout, a public prosecutor in the Johannesburg Children's Court;
- Captain Colin Morris, District Chief of the Randburg Family Violence and Sexual Assault Unit;
- Dr Lorna Jacklin, who trains doctors to examine sexually abused children;
- Luke Lampbrecht, who embodies dedication to this cause; and

All the councellors who dedicate their time and emotion to helping abused children.

These are the giants who help our children pick up that sword, stand behind them and say "I will help you slay this dragon".

To my partner, Vanessa Wilson, who believes in what I do and always supports me in my efforts.

And to my children, Themba and Khangiswa, who show me that life really is not that serious …

Contents

Sum of my story

The churning in my stomach tells me it's close to the last bell – I hate this time of day. When the bell rings it's the end of school for today. My heart is beating faster, because I know that even if he is not there sitting on the wall opposite the school to fetch my brother and me, he will be at home when I get there.

My heart feels painful, as if it's being pushed through a shredder. I feel suffocated; I can't get enough air into my lungs. The whole sky turns grey when I come out of the building and see him sitting there. He gives me that horrible smile that he seems to keep only for me. I make sure my brother is close to me and walks on one side and he, the pig, on the other. I can feel the sun burn down on my neck, but the burning inside of me is much stronger and more real. I can feel it growing like a bonfire inside. I remember last year when I was seven, the gardener made this big fire of leaves and sticks, and we put on more and more sticks until the colours turned red and golden and the sparks flew into the sky. I can feel I'm putting more and more hate onto this fire inside me and some time it will swallow up the pig and burn him to death, or else it will consume me.

I'm only a child, but already I am a worrier. I wonder if he does bad things to my brother too. Maybe he does it when I'm asleep? I don't think so, because I've taught myself to wake up at the smallest sound. But what if he does and my brother is also carrying this shameful secret on his shoulders? He is only a baby; but I think as long as I make the pig look at me, it will distract him and he will not fiddle with my brother.

He takes my schoolbag from me and carries it. Then he puts his hand on my neck and rubs it gently. To a passerby, it looks like a sign of affection, but I understand the unspoken innuendo. He moves his hand in circles, the way he does on my inner thighs.

I've been suffering this for almost three years now, and I know no one will believe me if I tell them. He tells me that all the time – that I'm the seducer, and, anyway, no one will believe me. He's my father's best friend and we share a house with him; it's not easy to tell on him. I know he is also abusing two other girls whose fathers play cards with him in the evenings, and they too are afraid. For a child, it's a most terrible place to be – when you know something is wrong, but you know you won't be believed.

I've managed to find a 'happy place' inside my head, a refuge where I can go, where none of this is real. I often go there during school time as well, and my teachers get very frustrated and yell at me for day-dreaming. But it's the only place where I feel safe.

I dream of puppies licking my face; I concentrate on the smell of puppy breath. Or I imagine the silence at the bottom of the swimming pool; cool, murky water above me, where it's just me and the water. And sometimes I try being like that armadillo I saw in a book of strange and wonderful animals. It can curl into a little ball and no one can open it up; it can roll over any terrain and stay for as long as it wants to in that position.

I don't know why I endured it for so long. One night I decided – I don't know where it came from – but I decided enough was enough. I waited until he had penetrated me and then I began to scream at the top of my lungs. My father came running into the room, and he lost control completely. There was an ugly scene, with lots of shouting and swearing and my father punched the pig. For the first time I heard raw tones in my father's voice. It was the one and only time he stood up for me.

From that day on I never forgot the power of my voice. I would later teach other children to use this power, at the Teddy Bear Clinic[1] where I worked as a volunteer for many years. At this centre I prepared children going to court to testify against their abusers. I lived vicariously through

---

[1]   www.ttbc.org.za

them as I never got the chance to do that for myself … using the power that speaking up brings. I have trained many paramedics in the pre-hospital recognition of suspected child abuse and how to deal with it. Those experiences have taught me the importance of touch, the way you hold a patient, the way your voice conveys a no-nonsense command. I have learnt that children are not little adults, and that they have a voice that must be heard.

Introduction

I walk up the familiar stairs at the Old Transvaal Memorial Institute in Braamfontein on my way to the Teddy Bear Clinic. This is the original children's hospital in Johannesburg and these same stairs were walked by the infamous Daisy de Melker[2]. They were also traversed by many of the paramedics[3] who were taught in Johannesburg when the old Johannesburg Ambulance Training College was still in existence.

I walked these stairs for fifteen years, on the second Saturday of every month. While still a volunteer here, I facilitated the parents' group. These were the parents of children who had been abused – mostly sexually – and I prepared them for facing the ordeal of their appearance in court.

---

[2]   http://en.wikipedia.org/wiki/Daisy_de_Melker
[3]   I am a qualified ALS paramedic who has been in Emergency Services since 1989, now working as a remote-site paramedic.

To me, the sights and sounds are welcomingly familiar – the same old brightly coloured walls, the same rickety lift, the old diamond-shaped windows. I volunteered in this old building for so long, first as a Childline councellor and then as a Teddy Bear Clinic councellor and facilitator, that walking the same old stairs, taking the same rickety lift is like coming home.

Nothing can prepare a parent for hearing that their child has been abused. Whether the information comes from the child or someone else, the news is devastating. It's difficult for parents to accept that, yes, this terrible thing has happened to their child. It is an awful thing; I cannot offer any explanation about why it happened to their or anyone's child. But the fact that they, as parents, are there at the clinic today, means they are part of a process that they have bravely decided to embark on. And they must never underestimate their presence in this process, it's invaluable – they may not see the rewards immediately, but I promise you in the end it will bear fruit for both them and their child.

As clichéd as it sounds, I often told them: Your children are the lucky ones – they are getting the chance to come to court and tell their story, irrespective of sentencing. There are hundreds of children who will never be believed by their parents and hundreds more whose mothers will silently collude with the father and look the other way, for various reasons. Many more children will never see the inside of a courtroom because of cultural differences, distance, bribery, intimidation by the perpetrator's family, and so on.

It is incredibly empowering for a child to be able to tell their story, to hear their parents say "I believe you, I stand by you, let's see how we can make this better." I am not naïve enough to try to convince you that the perpetrator is definitely going to be found guilty because these schedule-six offences are difficult to try in a courtroom. I will discuss the problems that arise on the legal side later on.

For now, for me as a non-religious person, spending a full four hours preparing and empowering parents going to court is as close to a religious experience as one can find.

I watch the women who volunteer to work with the children. It's by no means an easy task to get a group of three-, four- and five-year-olds together, even under ordinary circumstances. But when they've all been damaged by having a sacred boundary crossed, and you now need to prepare them for the legal process, it's truly a major operation.

I am humbled by the women who give up one Saturday a month to come and make coffee and sandwiches; they choose not to counsel but still want to do their bit.

I am in awe of Agnes, a public prosecutor in the children's court, who sat in on my group with me and patiently answered the parents' questions concerning legal issues. Here is someone who could so easily give up this job and go into the private sector. She would work better hours and receive far more remuneration – and yet her heart is here. Who says angels don't walk among us?

I see my colleague Colin, a reservist Child Protection Unit member who also selflessly gives up one of his Saturday mornings to help parents understand what happens after a docket is opened.

I was privileged to work with these selfless, dedicated councellors. And the inestimable reward was having children put their trust in us.

All the children who come to the Teddy Bear Clinic have been abused in one way or another, but mostly sexually. So let's begin there – how does this happen? How can someone we all know so well be an abuser – who are these people? How do our children become susceptible? And what can we do to support our children?

I'll endeavour to answer all these questions so that, by the time you have finished this book, you will be well informed. For some of you reading this book it will be too late, as the terrible deed has already been done and you are seeking answers. For others, it might be that you are a parent or a teacher and you choose to buy a book like this to enable you to make informed decisions should such a horrible situation arise. And then there are those who were abused at some point in their lives and still seek answers for that eternal emotional undercurrent that flows in them.

CHAPTER 1

The typical abused child

Much of this book's content is geared to telling it like it is and not sugar-coating the facts. So you might be surprised to hear things that don't sound right to you, and it is essential for me to try to dispel some myths.

MYTH: The child who is an introvert will be abused

This is not true at all. A child – whether they are introverted or not – who is taught about their body, who has an open relationship with their parents, and who has a healthy sense of self-confidence will not allow a paedophile to touch them. In fact, such a child is a threat to a paedophile. Bear in mind that a paedophile will want to use the child over and over again. So a child who is clued up and educated – even if they are introverted – will not be afraid to say, "don't do that!" The paedophile will stay well away from being exposed by such a child.

MYTH: Paedophiles use extreme force to abuse children

Cases in which a child has been abducted and raped and dragged through the veldt, and is sometimes found dead, are usually a once-off thing. These are acts done on the spur of the moment by criminals who are sometimes under the influence of drugs or alcohol, have no self-control, and are impulsive. This is not your everyday child abuse.

More often, paedophiles want to be able to use the child over a period of time – to even swap children if they are part of a syndicate – so no, violence is seldom used. Violence in syndicates does exist but this is the exception, not the rule.

For instance, 'The Wonderland Bust[4]', a syndicate bust that happened in the United Kingdom and was then found to span eighteen countries, was a syndicate that did use violence. The difference was that these children were run-aways and often drugged. What made the bust so alarming was that Scotland Yard discovered that paedophiles were using sophisticated equipment, like webcams, and then logging on in different countries and telling the paedophile in a room with one child or more, what to do to the child, as if they were there. This organisation had been using web-cams long before they were on sale to the public! What made

---

[4]   As reported in the UK newspaper, *The Sun*.

this bust so devastating was that to join the syndicate a potential member had to submit 10,000 original photos of themselves abusing a child – not posing – it had to be the real thing!

Most paedophiles typically spend a lot of time gaining the child's trust and making the child feel special and 'heard'. This is part of the paedophile's grooming process, which allows them ongoing access to the child. You will find out more about grooming in the next chapter.

Finally, not all paedophiles are 'out there' – often they live in our homes. These paedophiles have no need for force; instead, their control is much more subtle and insidious. But more about that later...

Children most at risk of abuse

The typically-abused child is the child who falls into any one of these high-risk groups:

1. **Mothers with multiple partners**. The most common type of sexual abuse reported is between a father and a daughter, followed by stepfather-daughter, followed by grandfather-granddaughter. The most unreported are mother-son abuse and sibling incest. Mothers who have many boyfriends are definitely placing their children in the high-risk category. These children are used to fend- ing for themselves, accustomed to short relationships,

and grow up really quickly. These children want a normal family with a mom and a dad, and thus try very hard to please.

2. **Runaways**. These children are at the mercy of anyone on the street who shows them some kindness. As a paramedic who worked in Hillbrow for fifteen years, I met many young girls who had Nigerian pimps. The story was always the same – they had an unbearable home life, were being abused by their mother and/or father/stepfather, so they ran away to Hillbrow. Here they were picked up by a pimp who befriended them and promised to give them a place to sleep and to take care of them. The first week would be bliss; she'd be taken out, they'd go clubbing, he'd buy her clothes and feed her. After that it wasn't so blissful because he'd drug her and she'd become hooked. Then followed a vicious cycle of trying to come off the drugs, and the only solution these children could find was to sell their bodies. They'd do this for their pimp, as he'd 'own' them. Other runaways sometimes become victims of those once-off, violent killings you read about. America is full of them; one only has to log on to the site for missing and exploited children, which is a link on the FBI website, to see how many children have ended up missing after having run away.

3. **Children moving from one foster home to another or children who are in orphanages or special homes**. This is a sad reality as these children are already so vulnerable.

They are in a system that is grossly understaffed and the screening process is just not strict enough. This attracts suspiciously-motivated people to work as hostel mothers or fathers; they are attracted to jobs where they have easy access to many children. These children are young and usually have very low self-esteem. Often they've been abandoned or removed from home at an early age, so a sense of belonging is missing and they are at incredibly high risk.

4. **Children who are handicapped and cannot articulate**. These children are an obvious high risk. No one can forget the vivid images on Carte Blanche of an old man being smacked around in an old age home by the 'caregiver'. Can you imagine a handicapped child? I don't need to elaborate on this point. In families, there is sometimes a child whom the family will gang up on and pick on; the weakling, the one with a stutter, the child with a small deformity. This is not unusual and many books have been written about such cases. Books such as *Ugly* by Constance Brenner and *A Child Called It* by David Pelzer are classic examples of this category of child. There is a 'silent collusion' on the part of all the family members, with siblings either torn between allowing it to happen so that it doesn't happen to them, or being too scared to confront the situation and split up the family. This has enormous repercussions for those siblings when they grow up. Evidence shows that they tend to gravitate towards substance abuse or other

destructive coping mechanisms, blaming themselves for allowing the abuse to carry on. But there are also cases in which the abuse brought siblings closer together in later years.

5. **Children with poor self-esteem or low self-confidence:** These children generally seek approval from others, lack the confidence to stand up for themselves, and find it difficult to say "No". Almost all the environments covered in risk categories 1 to 4 are perfect breeding grounds for poor self-esteem and feelings of not being good enough. Children from so-called 'normal' households or two-parent homes can just as easily become victims if they lack self-esteem and seek validation. Paedophiles prey on this weakness, recognising that these children are more open to spoiling and receiving attention, affirmation and affection.

6. **Children who are frequently left unattended:** Paedophiles are quick to spot children whose parents appear to be 'absent'; perhaps they habitually pick their children up late after school or sports; or they leave their children unsupervised during the afternoons. This gives the paedophile ample opportunity to befriend the child and start the grooming process (see Chapter 2).

It must be remembered that the subject of child abuse is not a black and white picture – there are no absolutes. That is what makes working in this arena so challenging.

Detecting abuse

Detecting child abuse is a difficult task because child abuse shares symptoms with other problems. For instance, a disruptive child with a bruise on his arm is not necessarily being abused.

When you know what signs and symptoms to look for, you will find they appear in combinations rather than as single signs. In addition, you need to weigh up signs in context. As a paramedic I have been to situations where I have found a baby sleeping in a tomato box, but that baby was well fed and the parent was worried enough to phone the ambulance because of his fever. I have also been to calls where a child had great difficulty breathing because the parent didn't buy the child her medication. That is a form of neglect; that child depends on the parent for its medication. So, what at first seems like a dyspnoea attack, is, in reality, also a case of neglect.

Here are some of the ways that children are abused, as well as signs and symptoms to look out for.

Physical abuse or neglect
- Burn marks from cigarettes
- Whipping marks by objects such as coat hangers, a *sjambok* (heavy whip)
- Lashings with heavy objects
- Bruising in various places and in different stages of healing

- Fractures in various stages of healing
- Dislocations
- Injuries to the mouth
- Tying the child up or restraining them for long periods
- Locking the child in a cupboard
- Pulling hair and limbs
- Starving the child
- Not giving the child necessary medication
- Shaken baby syndrome – small children usually younger than one years old may show signs of a floppy head, sleepiness, lapses in and out of consciousness, and bruising on their shoulders where they have been held and shaken violently.
- Wearing long-sleeved clothes in hot weather or wearing many clothes when unnecessary.

Sexual abuse
- Foul-smelling or frequent discharge
- Blood on underwear
- Excessive smell of adult sweat on a small child
- Blood, pain, itching, swelling or redness in the genital area
- Abnormal way of walking
- Not wanting to sit properly
- Vaginal or penile infections
- Missing of periods
- Sexually transmitted diseases
- Early pregnancy
- Urinary tract infections – children who are examined by

the District Surgeon are placed on anti-retroviral drugs – this is the harsh reality of sexual abuse of children. I have had parents in my group share the devastating news that their six-year-old has contracted AIDS due to the abuse.

How children may react

It goes without saying that emotional and psychological abuse accompanies physical and sexual abuse. It affects the milestones of small children, and when they are a little older they will display a wider range of behavioural signs.

When a child is very young, the only defence they have is to yell. Trust me, as a paramedic it's very distressing trying to get near a child who is yelling at you. When they are very young, in times of stress – even natural stress like the birth of a new sibling who usurps their position as the baby – children display regressive behaviour. This can include bedwetting and talking or screaming in their sleep. Bear in mind that as the child gets older, their anger is expressed in a greater number of ways. Teenagers are particularly difficult. Already they are at a stage in their lives where they are not yet adults but no longer children. This period of life is stressful enough as they try to find themselves through a hormone-haze. Now you have a teenager who has been violated. They can display a range of emotions that can really push your buttons, make you despair and drive you to drink – but please don't.

Behavioural signs in children can include:

- learning problems: difficulties at school and lack of interest in creative activities and play
- difficulty remembering and concentrating
- regressive language and body movement
- regressive behaviour – biting or kicking other children
- attention-seeking behaviour
- depressive states like sadness, anxiety, agitation
- eating disorders like vomiting and refusing to eat
- isolation from other children of the same age
- fear of adults or of the parent of the same sex as the abuser
- avoiding certain people, rooms in a house or places
- ambivalence towards the teacher and/or other children that was not there before
- precocious and provocative sexual behaviour towards children of the same age or adults
- unusual recognition of sexual terminology for their age
- excessive masturbating in class
- sleep disturbances such as recurring nightmares, talking, or screaming in their sleep
- psychosomatic pain, such as stomach aches
- running away from school
- breaking things
- hurting animals and/or people
- setting fire to objects
- trying to push boundaries by deliberately doing something they know is not allowed; for instance, if their room is usually tidy, they will make it messy to provoke

you to see what you will do: will you, who love them, also hurt them?
- overly submissive or overly compliant behaviour, trying to be the 'perfect child'
- withholding affection
- a lack of boundaries, such as purposely invading siblings' rooms, stealing other childrens' stuff, and so on.

In older children and teenagers, signs may be the same but can also include:
- an increase in day-dreaming, lying on a sofa or bed for hours just not doing anything, apathetic attitude
- not keeping clean; their personal hygiene starts to deteriorate because they want to make themselves ugly and smelly so no one else will come near them
- difficulty trusting others, sometimes deliberately sabotaging friendships
- guilt
- starving themselves or over-eating as a form of punishment or to appear unattractive
- neurotic habits, such as washing hands frequently and excessive bathing or showering
- missing school
- breaking and destroying objects, even school property
- feelings of isolation, not participating in group activities, reclusiveness
- anxiety and/or depression
- feelings of suicide
- outbursts of anger and irrational crying episodes

- deliberately staying out late
- deliberately invading other people's space, not knocking before entering a room as they usually would
- smoking
- taking drugs, alcohol abuse
- frequently buying new underwear
- mutilating their body by burning or cutting themselves. This is very distressing behaviour for a parent to deal with. Indeed, it will very often not be known from the start, as cutters usually become adept at hiding the cutting marks and hurt themselves in areas that are hidden by clothing, like the inside of their forearms, on their stomachs or their thighs. Cutters are not seeking attention – far from it. It is a way of feeling relief. The ritual leading up to the act is something they have total control over – they feel empowered. Some teenagers feel so numb that the slight pain of cutting makes them feel alive, normal. Seeing the blood affirms that they are the same as everyone else; so, it's done because they don't feel as if they belong any more. They feel dirty, they feel as if they have been singled out because of who they are. A bad thing was done to them because they themselves are bad. I suggest reading the most excellent book ever written on this subject, *A Bright Red Scream* by Marilee Strong.

CHAPTER 2

The grooming process

All criminals have two things in common: they lack self-control and they are opportunistic, meaning that they will seize the opportunity to commit a crime when that opportunity presents itself. This applies to child molesters and paedophiles – whether it's a once-off attack where violence is used, a premeditated process that involves grooming the child over a period of time, or a father molesting his own child.

The heinous act of sexually abusing children is an act of self-gratification. The abuser knows that he or she is doing something that is not only unlawful, but also unacceptable to society in general. They are committing an act that is not a reaction to anger, or an act of seeking justice or revenge – it is a one-sided, opportunistic, selfish act; an act usually performed behind closed doors, in secret. With sexual abuse, it is seldom that other children are witnesses to the actual abuse except, for example, in extreme cases where groups of children are filmed or photographed by paedophiles who are part of a syndicate, and where the abuse may be captured in real time and sent via live streaming to other paedophiles around the world. Witnessed sexual abuse can sometimes happen when the abuser uses the act to instil fear and manipulate the victims into complying, as in Satanic cults.

So exactly how does a paedophile 'groom' a child? How does a paedophile get a child from the point where the child doesn't know them to the point where the child is dependent and guilt-ridden and having sexual relations with them?

There are two primary categories of abuse: extrafamilial abuse and intrafamilial abuse. Extrafamilial abuse is abuse that occurs outside of the family: the perpetrators are non-family members and may or may not be known to the child. These perpetrators may abuse the child just once, or could engage in a grooming process to gain the child's trust with a view to abusing the child on an ongoing basis. Intrafamilial abuse, on the other hand, occurs within the family. The perpetrator could be a direct family member, an extended member, or a step-member, such as a step-father or brother.

Extrafamilial abuse

The total stranger

This abuser is someone who has had limited or no prior contact or interaction with the child and the abuse will very often, though not always, be a one-off event. The abuser is not interested in establishing a long-term relationship with the child – the abuse is opportunistic in nature – so no grooming is necessary. The abuser usually uses trickery to lure their child victims; for instance, they may stop and ask the child to show them where the nearest cafe is, ask the child to help them find their missing dog, or knock on the front door and ask to use the phone if they know the child is home alone. Once they have the child's attention and initial co-operation, this type of abuser tends to control the child through coersion, confrontation, threats of force, and physical force if necessary. This type of attack can sometimes turn into the really violent, even fatal kind of attack you read about in newspapers.

The groomer

The process used by this type of paedophile is very well thought out. You have to understand that the paedophile (applies to females as well) is the most cunning animal walking this earth; they are masters of manipulation.

The longer a paedophile has been abusing children, the cleverer they become at the grooming process. They know that what they are doing is wrong and spend a lot of time covering their tracks. Let me begin by explaining how the process works.

Let's, for the purposes of this book, have an imaginary scenario. This could apply to boys or girls participating in any sport, or Boy Scouts/Girl Guides, or any activities in which children engage in groups. In our example, Frank is a soccer coach. It is the beginning of the season and he has a whole new squad of boys who have joined the club. Now Frank is going to pick out a boy he wants to abuse. How does he make this choice? It's not going to be the shy, introverted boy, nor will it be the bully. He looks for the needy child, the one who is ignored at home, the child who doesn't have a good relationship with his parents, the child whose parents are 'absent' and don't seem interested.

How does Frank figure this out? One of the tell-tale signs is the child whose parents never come and watch him play soccer, or the child whose parents continually fetch him late, long after the game has ended. This tells Frank many things; the parents are not that interested in the child or they are not pro-active parents. The child will be left to do a lot of things on his own, and he has a deep need for a 'friend,' someone who is interested in him, who will acknowledge him as a person and make him feel important. This is the first step in the grooming process – the choice of victim.

The next step is to start to single out the child, make him feel special, wanted, acknowledged as a favorite boy. This is very intoxicating to a child who isn't used to being made to feel remarkable in any way. He looks forward to going to soccer practice; he relishes the attention. When Frank talks to him, he speaks to him like an adult, never degrades him or makes him feel silly or unwanted.

The next step is one of the most important in the grooming process; Frank gets to meet the parents. This is pivotal in the process as it is the parents who are the end of the line, if a charge is to be laid. The confidence of the parents must be earned, just as much as that of the victim. How many times have you seen the headlines: "He was liked by everyone", "a pillar of the community," just like Gert van Rooyen. He was a member of the Pretoria Chamber of Commerce, was a deacon in his church, held Sunday school at his house … In other words, he was constantly surrounded by children where their presence wasn't questioned.

Frank will ingratiate himself into the boy's family, making a point of getting to know them well. He'll pop in often, sometimes have dinner with them; the neighbours will also get to know who Frank is. Even the dogs in the house will be used to him. I remember in one of my court prepping sessions a mother told me that she had even allowed the suspect neighbour to bath her kids! Frank gets on well with the parents, making it very difficult later for the child to tell on him, fearing his parents will not believe him because they know and like Frank.

In the next step, Frank starts to take away responsibilities from the parents. This has a two-fold effect: the parents start to unconsciously depend on Frank, and it affirms how 'wonderful' he is. He will start phoning the parents and suggesting he come and fetch the boy for practice. Next thing he will be fetching him and taking him home.

Then, he will start to buy the child gifts. This entrenches in the child's mind how outstanding he is in Frank's eyes, and here begins the 'first secret' that might be suggested. Frank will tell him that he really wants to buy him a new pair of boots, but he feels that maybe the parents might not approve. Invariably, the gift will be so enticing that the child's response will be: "I won't tell!" This is important because the child was the first one to say it. And once the first secret has begun, it will be one of many between them. Usually the parents are either so absent that they don't notice these gifts, or they are so impressed that Frank takes such an interest in their son, they will be grateful, even proud.

Frank will continue to buy the young boy more gifts and will then introduce the concept of giving him money. This allows the child to start depending on Frank. They could even reach the point where he might ask for more because he is very comfortable with Frank. This entrenches the bond between Frank and the young boy; sharing secrets is a very powerful element in the grooming process.

The next step takes place when Frank introduces his living space to the young boy. He knows the child is curious, and he reinforces his hold by using sentences like: "You can always come here, you can leave your stuff here – it will be safe." Very often there will be a Playstation and typical children's stuff that the child might not have at home. Sometimes he will make a big show of clearing a shelf or a drawer and say things like: "This is your drawer, no-one else will use this drawer." The seed has been planted, the young boy now has a place to come to, a place where he can escape, a place where he is exceptional…

So now Frank is supplying the young boy with money, giving him gifts, and taking him to his house or living space so often that the youngster is comfortable there. Then follows more freedom. He allows the child to do things in this space that he is not allowed to do at home. He may watch as much TV as he wants, smoke grass, drop some acid, take E, and importantly, Frank even has parties at his house that lots of boys come to.

Let's recap for a moment. Here was a child with very little self-confidence, not acknowledged by his parents. Now he is important because other boys want to come to these parties. He is somebody, he is elevated amongst his peers, and he has a connection. He has moved from zero to hero – very powerful indeed. What is disturbing is that very often the boys who come to these parties don't even play soccer with Frank.

Nudity is also common now. The late Lawrence Katz, Deputy Director of Johannesburg Emergency Services, who was arrested for sexual relations with minors, had many boys come to his house and would hold parties in his jacuzzi. He was also a scout master. Young boys are very taken in by uniforms, which exemplify a sense of power, elevating the paedophile even more. Petrus van Wyk, Deputy Principal of Randburg High School, was another paedophile in a prominent position who had 22 charges of abuse against him. He, too, used parties and nudity in the grooming process.

Next, Frank introduces his body to the child. He does this in a very non-threatening manner. For example, he might say that he hurt his knee at soccer practice and he needs a massage. This is the first time that the child is asked to do something for Frank. The boy will agree, and feels important that he can reciprocate Frank's generosity, even if it involves physical interaction. So begins the first touching experience. This becomes a repeated action and the boy may even start offering to massage Frank's knee when he hears Frank complaining about it. The child is becoming comfortable with Frank's body, and Frank's nudity is accepted, normal behaviour around the house. This is exactly what Frank wants.

Pornography will be introduced and becomes a normal fixture in Frank's place. This is a powerful tool in the grooming process. It breaks down defences and sexualises young boys, capitalising on their raging hormones and natural curiousity about sex. The paedophile knows the boy is aroused.

The next step will be that Frank will molest the child when the youngster is not fully conscious. He can use a variety of substances to sedate the young boy, such as over-the-counter anti-histamines and alcohol. Then he will molest the boy to gauge his reaction.

One of two things can happen: the youngster realises what is going on and resists, decides to never go back, tells his parents he does not want to play soccer any more and keeps his secret. In a society where boys are supposed to be tough, it's very difficult for him to tell his peers that he was taken advantage of by Frank. His parents won't believe him as they love Frank. How many times have you read stories about men who've lived with the shameful secret of abuse by a priest or a teacher, and they couldn't tell their parents? I cannot emphasise enough how important it is to have an open relationship with your children so that they feel they can come and tell you anything.

The other option for the child is to stay because the parties, the endless supply of money, and the fun times with Frank will come to an end if he doesn't. It's not an easy decision – he weighs up what he will have to give up. But he's kept so many secrets with Frank for so long, he thinks he can continue – and he does.

The process of grooming kids is based on an imbalance of power – while the paedophile is grooming the boy, he is tipping the balance of power in his favour.

When I was at the Teddy Bear Clinic, and I recounted the steps in the grooming process, all around me I saw parents who nodded their heads or openly say: "That's exactly what he did!" The lights came on and they realised how powerful the grooming process is, how guilt-ridden the child feels, and why it is so difficult for the child to tell.

Intrafamilial abuse

This type of abuse is the most common, and the least reported. Here, the abuser is a family member. The onset of abuse is usually earlier and the duration of the abuse longer due to easy access to the child.

It is especially difficult to understand how a parent can abuse their own child. It is an act that transgresses sacred boundaries. The very person who is the child's hero, who can do no wrong, who is there to protect and guide the child, picking them up when they fall, and taking away their pain, is the very one who is giving them pain, making them feel sad, unsure, unsafe, confused, scared and forced into keeping a 'bad' secret. We must not forget that the paedophile *always* has the upper hand as there exists a gross imbalance of power – weight, body size, authority, knowledge and experience of the world – another reason why the secret is kept by the child.

Intrafamilial paedophiles already have the child's trust, and so the process of coercing the victim to participate in 'games' and keeping secrets is not fraught with having to win over the parents, getting the child to implicitly trust them, and other steps in the grooming process adopted by paedophiles not initially known to the child. They don't have to lure the child into being alone with them, as opportunities are already plentiful.

A common method used on very young children is to make the child believe that they did not experience the actual abuse. For example, the father will fondle the child when they are asleep; if the child awakes the child might feel fuzzy-headed, confused, and may think that they were dreaming. Sometimes the father might read a bedtime story while stroking the child; as the child falls asleep the father continues stroking and exploring other areas of the child's body. As the abuse progresses, the abuser's need for more interactive participation escalates to where all kinds of ruses are used. One of the parents I was prepping for court told me that the first time she witnessed her father convulsing, she was only four years old, and it was naturally very stressful for her. When her father started abusing her, he told her that she was his special girl, that she had magical powers, and that if she fellated him, he would not get these 'devil dances'. When she grew older she would sometimes refuse, and her enraged father would have a full-on seizure from the anger he felt. This affirmed to her that she was bad, she was facilitating this, that it was her fault, and "look what you have done, if you had only made Daddy feel good, the devil would not have made me dance". This continued right up until she was a teenager and witnessed a young girl in her class at high school have a seizure just like her father's. The teacher then explained what epilepsy was. This is a classic example of just how powerful suggestion is when it is enmeshed in a devious way to win the child over. Fathers may use sentences like "all daddies love their little princesses this way", "see how good you are at this", "you do this so well", "you are such a good girl", "you are the best", and "you make Daddy so happy when you do this special rub". Bribes are often used with older children, but the most common ploy is 'our secret'. The child is made to feel very special that she is keeping this secret. She is often rewarded for keeping it and does not want to disappoint her father by refuting his advances or denying him when the 'play' escalates. Games like tickling can be a precursor to abuse, and is used to gauge the child's reaction to being touched.

41

Men who abuse their own children tend to be over-protective. They rule the house with authority that is never questioned. They are very often the breadwinner and may capitalise on this while grooming the child, instilling in the child the fear that, if they report him, he will go to prison and they will live on the streets. These families often have blurred boundaries and there may be a reversal of roles; for instance, the older daughter takes on the role of the mother, and vice versa. A very strong patriarchal system is entrenched, and these families often become isolated from mainstream society. The most common threat is that the child believes that no one else will believe them.

It's not surprising that children who have been abused by a parent or family member often tell a friend rather than the other (non-abusing) parent. But this can present a problem in Court because this first testimony is the only testimony that can be presented as evidence, apart from what the victim says. Telling an adult later may not be used at the Court hearing because it is viewed as hearsay evidence. Fortunately, this is in the process of being changed.

Also, disclosure by very young children tends to be frag-mented as they don't have a clear idea of consecutive time and place. So, if a six-year-old tells another six-year-old, it can be a huge problem obtaining a statement that is concise and clear, and the defence will have a field day. Children also find it hard to understand family connections, for instance, that their father has a father; they only know him as granddad. It is also imperative to remember that some children love the perpetrator but not the deed – and for them, the two are very difficult to separate. It is also especially hard for children to disclose when the abuser is an authority figure and holds great power, social standing, and wears a uniform, such as a priest. More information about dealing with disclosure can be found in Chapter 5.

CHAPTER 3

The abuser

The APA's *Diagnostic and Statistical Manual of Mental Disorders* 4th edition, Text Revision, gives the following as its 'Diagnostic criteria for 302.2 Paedophilia':

- A. Over a period of at least six months, recurrent, intense sexually arousing fantasies, sexual urges, or behaviours involving sexual activity with a pre-pubescent child or children (generally aged thirteen or younger)

- B. The person has acted on these sexual urges, or the sexual urges or fantasies cause marked distress or interpersonal difficulty

- C. The person is at least sixteen years old and at least five years older than the child or children in Criterion A.

That is the definition in the DSM – the 'Bible' used by psychologists and psychiatrists to categorise patients.[5]

The important thing to remember is that there is **gross inequality** in the sexual abuse of children:

A) Power difference
B) Knowledge difference
C) Gratification difference

It has been observed that sex offenders generally lack the capacity for empathy. Despite the variety of treatment modalities, one of the central goals in all adolescent sexual offender programmes is the development of empathy for the victim. The following excerpt was taken from *When Young Children Molest Other Children* by Shaheda Omar, a child-play therapist at the Teddy Bear Clinic.

"This is becoming a worldwide phenomenon, the problem of young children perpetrating sexual crimes on other young children. Numerous studies have documented the

---

[5] Now, before all those who hold Masters and PhDs attack me and explain that there are many categories that paedophiles fall into, please remember that this book is aimed at the lay person who simply wants the gist of it and doesn't want to wade through dissertations and technicalities. I acknowledge that there is a difference between child molesters and incestuous and non-incestuous paedophiles, which is an American definition. There have been many men and women who have studied paedophiles and even found physical differences such as their having a smaller hypothalamus. However; this book is intended simply to inform and give a better understanding of this heinous behaviour to prepare and help people should it ever happen in their circle.

high prevalence of early sexual victimisation in the history of adolescent offenders. Psychiatric comorbidity has been found to exist in 60%–90% of adolescent sex offenders. The most prevalent of these disorders are: conduct disorders (45%–80%), mood disorders (35%–50%), substance abuse (20%–30%), and attention deficit hyperactivity disorder (10%–20%)." (Houghughi, 1997, Shaw et al, 1999).

I pose a question to you before I discuss the various types of paedophiles out there. I cannot argue with the studies, but consider this: The statistics tell us that one in three girls is abused before the age of five and one in five boys. So why aren't there more girls out there abusing other children?

One must be very careful not to assume that because something was done to you, you will automatically do it to someone else. This is a myth perpetuated by the tabloids who have clearly not looked at the statistics. It also leads to the type of thinking that gives us the classic defence excuse in court. We are accustomed to seeing defence attorneys strutting in their black gowns and spouting forth statements like, "We can understand why my client sodomises boys; he was sodomised when he was a youngster." And so the perpetrator comes to be seen as a victim, an object of pity and not the criminal he really is. The greatest threat to society, as far as I am concerned, is the normalisation of abnormal or unacceptable behaviour. It is the very process that anaesthetises us as human beings.

I'm not saying that bad experiences in childhood don't have a bearing on one's life later. Of course, it's inevitable that there would be after-effects, to say the least. But how one deals with it, the support of the family, the ability to discuss it, the fact that you were believed – all these factors have a huge impact on the child and how that child will behave as an adult. Certainly, it's a fact that not all children who were abused go on to become paedophiles! Offenders know the difference between right and wrong. One must remember that paedophiles are criminals, cunning and manipulative criminals. They have what all criminals have in common – lack of self control and the ability to create opportunities.

Basically, there are three types of paedophiles:
1.   The regressive
2.   The immature
3.   The fixated

The regressive paedophile

The regressive paedophile is someone who usually abuses members of his own family. He abuses in times of crisis as he doesn't have the coping skills to deal with emergencies. He is normally married and has a very immature way of dealing with problems. For instance, if the family dog dies he will quickly buy another one because he cannot deal with the emotional aspect of grieving. They usually start abusing in their late twenties or early thirties. This is when the wife or partner might leave; there could be a divorce and he is either left with the children or he has them for week-ends and holidays. He cannot deal with this crisis, and is constantly in victim mode. He slowly but surely pushes the young girl to take on more and more responsibilities around the house, replacing the absent mother.

Then it's on to "I am lonely in this big bed, come sleep with daddy". The young girl wants the recognition; if there are smaller siblings she is being treated differently. She might enjoy the attention, and will do whatever her father tells her. These types of paedophiles are very seldom caught because the abuse is literally kept in the family. Sometimes there is alcohol involved and/or drugs but there is definitely no direct correlation between substance abuse and regressive paedophile behaviour. The incidence of these offenders repeating the behaviour is very low.

Regressive paedophiles are typically treated using family systems therapy in which the entire family is placed in therapy together. The father is shown the error of his ways, and it is often the case that the abuse is a secondary factor, not a primary factor such as stress.

The immature paedophile

This type of child molester makes up the smallest percentage of paedophiles. These are adults who cannot interact with other adults, or certainly find it difficult to do so. They tend to be loners and often stay at home with their parents; they genuinely see children as people they are in love with. They will think a little girl who sits on his lap without a nappy or that kisses him is seducing him. These are individuals who have remained stuck at the childhood stage of development.

One sometimes finds severe learning difficulties among them. They have the same mental age as their victims.[6] Very often there is no sexual abuse but more hugging of the child or smothering the child with affection.

The fixated paedophile

This is the one that we need to fear. He normally starts abusing in his early twenties. He is sometimes married and has a family – as in the case of Gert van Rooyen[7] (a classic fixated paedophile). These people gravitate towards jobs where the presence of many children around them is not questioned. They often have jobs that require them to wear a uniform. They may also have a solid and important level in society, for instance teachers, priests, scout masters, and so on.

Nowadays, they normally have access to a computer, and some join syndicates – which I will discuss in the next chapter. They know that what they are doing is wrong and make great efforts to cover their tracks. If caught and subsequently released, the chances of repeating the same crime are great. They are not remorseful of their behaviour; they lack empathy. These paedophiles are not curable. Many experiments have taken place worldwide in treating

---

[6]   From the Innocence in Danger website, a UNESCO initiative against Internet paedophilia. See http://www.unesco.org/webworld/highlights/innocence_161099.html

[7]   http://en.wikipedia.org/wiki/Gert_van_Rooyen

paedophiles, and millions of dollars spent – including chemical castration, hormone treatment and behaviour modification – but to no avail.

It is sad to think that vast amounts of money are spent on trying to find a cure, but not even a third of that money is spent on the victims.

Molesters want to fulfill a need, and that is to appease their sexual gratification by whatever means. Simply put, it is a case of 'big bodies using little bodies for their own selfish needs.' They tend to have specific preferences regarding looks, for instance, blond with blue eyes. They also tend to go for a specific age group, not varying by more than two years either way. They are meticulous about collecting and storing information on the children they have abused. Before the days of the Internet, when these paedophiles were caught, it was not unusual to find copious notes written about the children. There were descriptions, names, dates, measurements of genitalia, likes and dislikes of the child, and so on. With the advent of the Internet it has, unfortunately, become more difficult to track them down. They swap information with other fixated paedophiles, as this affirms their behaviour and many organisations exist today that carry the banner of 'child and adult love'. This is simply a euphemistic name for having lustful intentions towards children. I will discuss different paedophile organisations next, some of which have been around for many years.

Paedophile organisations

This may be hard to read and seem unbelievable, but the facts show that organisations exist right under our noses and some of them want recognition for, as one organisation's banner reads, 'the love between an adult and a child' (www.martinj. org). All this information is available on the Internet. Pro-paedophile activism started in the early 1950s and continues today.

These organisations argue that what we consider harmful – being intimate with children – is, in fact, not harmful at all; rather, it is the years of social conditioning that make us hold that view; a collective condemnation by social conditioning, if you will. Writings about the effects of having sex with children and how it does not negatively impact on children date as far back as 1948–1952 in the Alfred Kinsey report in which Kinsey states that "all children are sexual from birth". Dr. Frits Bernard[8] was a psychologist and sexologist known for his outspoken views on various sexual taboos. He wrote a book called *Sex met Kinderen*, which was published in 1972 by a Dutch sexual reform organisation. This book had a great impact on the western European public and is considered the foundation of pro-paedophile activism organisations. Many of these organisations have tried, at various times, to align themselves with homosexual groups to gain recognition, but have often failed. The last attempt to do this was made by

---

[8]   http://www.ipce.info/ipceweb/Library/dutch_movement_text.htm

Vereniging MARTIJN, a Dutch organisation, in 1982 (www. martijn.org).

It is important to note that these pro-paedophile organisations have a few goals in common:

1. To redefine the meaning of sexual abuse, by using slogans like 'free acceptance of child and adult love' and using phrases like 'the child's consent';

2. Promoting the idea that children can consent to sexual activity with adults;

3. Questioning the assumption of harm between an adult and a 'consenting' child;

4. Declassification of paedophilia as a mental illness;

5. Promoting understanding of 'relationships';

6. Referring to experiences or situations where adult-child sex interactions are not illegal; both historical and anthropological;

7. Pointing to juvenile sexual activity in the animal kingdom historically, and invoking evolutionary arguments;

8. Arguing that inequality does not necessarily mean abuse;

9. Invoking ideas of continuity between paedophiles and other minority activists. Some activists argue that paedophile activism, feminism, gay activism, and anti-racism all relate to the experiences of suppressed and misunderstood groups;

10. Lowering the age of consent.

Here is a list of the better-known organisations:

- Danish Paedophile Association (or DPA Gruppe 04)
- Dutch Society for Sexual Reform
- Krumme 13
- North American Man/Boy Love Association (NAMBLA)
- Paedophile Information Exchange
- Paidika: The Journal of Paedophilia
- Partij voor Naastenliefde, Vrijheid en Diversiteit
- René Guyon Society
- Vereniging MARTIJN
- The Childhood Sensuality Circle

The René Guyon Society

The René Guyon Society is an American group that advocates sexual relationships with children. It was named after René Guyon, a former judge who served on the Supreme Court of Thailand for 30 years and who, apart from traditional judicial work, wrote on sexual ethics in his work *The Ethics of Sexual Acts*. This group started in the early sixties in California. A group of parents at a high school dance were discussing sex between children and adults and found they held the similar notion that it was not bad, that what René Guyon had to say in his books about 'much of today's ills in society are because children are not sexualised from an early age,' was true. They started the René Guyon Society. The recruiting slogan for this organisation was and still is: "Sex by eight or else too late." In their constitution, they advocate that "every child has a right to a normal sexual relationship with another adult or sibling and shall be aided in doing so by being supplied with contraceptive devices, to prevent venereal diseases." It is one of the oldest pro-paedophile organisations.

The North American Man/Boy Love Association (NAMBLA[9]) is a New York City and San Francisco-based unincorporated organisation in the USA, which already had 1,000 members in 1995. Formerly known as the IPCE (International Paedophile and Child Emancipation movement), they are a very outspoken and prominent organisation that advocates the liberalisation of laws against sexual relations between adult and minor males.

NAMBLA supports and promotes similar views held by many such organisations – to "end the oppression of men and boys who have freely chosen mutually consenting relationships". NAMBLA also calls for "the adoption of laws that both protect children from unwanted sexual experiences and at the same time leave them free to determine the content of their own sexual experiences."

NAMBLA's website claims that: "NAMBLA does not provide encouragement, referrals or assistance to people seeking sexual contacts" and that it does not "engage in any activities that violate the law [or] advocate that anyone else should [violate the law]".

---

[9]   www.nambla.org

NAMBLA holds an annual gathering in New York City and monthly meetings around the country. In the early 1980s, NAMBLA was reported to have had more than three hundred members, and was supported by such noted figures as Allen Ginsberg[10]. Since then, the organisation has kept membership data private, but an undercover FBI investigation in 1995 discovered that there were 1,100 members. It is the largest organisation in the umbrella group IPCE (formerly International Paedophile and Child Emancipation).

It is interesting to note also that many members of NAMBLA have been convicted of sexual offences against children. The disturbing thing is that recently an offshoot of this organisation called Butterfly Kisses has been formed, which is an organisation that professes love between older women and young girls.

www.martijn.org

This organisation, based in Holland, was started in 1982. Its banner on the opening page states "An organisation for the free acceptance of adult and child love". For the record, Berl Kutchinsky was commissioned by the United States to report on obscenity and pornography. He was professor of criminology, based in Denmark, which in 1969 became the first country to legalise pornography. Kutchinsky was in a

---

[10]   www.allenginsberg.org

unique position to study the effect of pornography on a massive scale. His findings caused great controversy as they did not support the previously held notion that legalising pornography would lead to an increase in sex crimes.

It goes without saying that the continuous lowering of the age of consent, and the perpetual images of adults and children in a sexual context, would, like most images, eventually desensitise us to it so that we are no longer conscious of it.

The book called *Lolita* by Vladimir Nabokov, published in the early 1950s, was banned in most countries because of its content. It tells the story of Hubert Humphries, an adult who falls in love with a 12-year-old girl. Some 50 years later, in 2000, it was listed as one of the 100 best reads, and in 1997, a remake of the film starring Jeremy Irons was widely acclaimed.

There is nothing wrong with adults reading books like this – what I am afraid of is parents becoming desensitised to the harm that paedophilia causes our children. We hear, read, and see so much that the material can lose its power to affect us. As a parent I am 'awake' to these organisations and the behaviour of paedophiles. Again, I stress this point: the normalisation of abnormal behaviour is a dangerous desensitising drug. It fogs our society in subtle ways. Through the media and beauty pageants, young girls are sexualised and portrayed in suggestive or sexy clothing. Well-known brands have even started producing sexy children's lingerie!

To this day, *Lolita* is still the largest-selling child pornography magazine, printed in Holland, followed by *Peach Fuzz, Lollytots,* and others, according to an investigation into child pornography conducted by Tim Tate for the BBC.

We must also be aware that we live in a country where it is customary to refer to an adult man as '*Oom*' (Uncle) and where children are told to "kiss that *Tannie* (Auntie)," whether they want to or not. We scold and pressurise our children for society's sake, but we are in fact contradicting our own dictum of, "Don't get into cars with strangers." This is known in psychology as a double bind. And many double binds and inconsistencies are dangerous and confusing to a child, causing huge internal conflict.

As a paramedic, I am sometimes aware of anomalies. We teach children to stay away from hot stoves where steam is coming out of a pot, but I must often tell a child who is struggling to breathe, to breathe through a mask with a fine mist coming out of it!

CHAPTER 4

Online predators and cyber bullying

In this day and age, where the Internet is part of daily life, parents can no longer afford to be left behind, claiming ignorance or resisting the need to keep up. The Internet is a powerful communication medium for youngsters to convey messages, connect with others, update their status, keep up with the latest news, and share photos and personal details. Unfortunately, this also leaves them wide open to the dangers associated with the Internet, such as cyber bullying and becoming victims of online sexual predators.

Facebook has become a way of life. Meeting at the mall is no longer as appealing as meeting new people online, uploading selfies, and perusing other peoples' albums – all from the safety of one's room. It is imperative that parents keep up with the digital age, educate themselves, and monitor the time that their children spend on the Net, as well as the sites that they visit. They must sit down with their kids and explain to them the dangers of distributing intimate information online. They need to warn them against sending strangers their private email or befriending anyone who will have access to their pictures and information. They must be particularly vigilant about handing out their personal address and contact details. They need to teach children how to create strong passwords to prevent unauthorised access to their social media and email accounts. This can be done in the context of 'playing a game', with the parent allowing the child to be the teacher. They need to be guided in choosing names and profile titles that are not suggestive. Using a webcam also creates a whole new gateway to another world and is the very instrument used to groom kids into doing more sinister things.

Parents need to research what Internet packages are out there to monitor the cyber traffic from the child's computer, track histories of websites visited, and block undesirable websites or websites that do not meet certain 'safe' criteria.

In South Africa, MXit, Myspace and Facebook are the more common social media platforms used. Youngsters are consumed with checking updates, sending pictures, text messages, Instant messaging, inviting friends and connecting to new friends in their quest to remain popular. Teenagers exist in a perpetual state of great emotion. They are not quite children, but also not quite adults. They will attempt to 'find themselves' in a way that can try the patience of many a parent. In their defence against their parents and the world, they invent new words and abbreviations that are widely used when texting each other. Teenagers often feel like they are on the outside, that no one understands them, and that they cannot communicate with their parents. This is exactly the type of void a cyber stalker and Internet groomer will fill. Children have little understanding that sharing your intimate thoughts is a very powerful weapon in the hands of paedophiles, cyber bullies and stalkers.

Where does Internet grooming happen?

The most common grooming ground for paedophiles is in chat rooms. Chat rooms enable you to have a conversation by way of typing rather than speaking. There can be more than one person in a chat room if it is an 'open' chat room or if you invite people to participate. Paedophiles also trawl social media sites, such as Facebook, to recruit children. They click on links that they see the teenager has an interest in. They start to befriend the teenager by having conversations with them and asking a few innocuous questions. The gaming arena is also very popular because here the paedophile knows what the child likes. The paedophile will ask to join the game or play against the child, or even ask to join their team if there is one, thus building a rapport. Parents need to be vigilant regarding their children's behaviour, taking care to notice signs such as a sudden influx of money, new clothes, withdrawal, odd phone calls, secretive behaviour, or the sudden switching off of their screens when you enter the room.

How does it happen?

Imagine a young girl who feels depressed because she has put on weight. She updates her mood message or social media profile to "Feeling sad". Her feelings, her state of mind, have now gone viral. She will elicit a reaction; people will post replies whether they are positive or negative, and whether they know her or not. It's a lifeline to anyone out there, a way of maintaining precious contact and receiving validation and acknowledgement. She feels 'out there'; alone. Her parents cannot communicate with her, they don't understand her. The paedophile befriends her, or is already a friend of a friend. He knows what she likes – what music she listens to, what books she has read, what her favourite movies are – as all this information is posted on her 'Likes' timeline. He could start a conversation asking her if she is going to see a certain movie, a band coming to town, and so on. He could start conversing with her about how he feels, how his weight depresses him, how he does not want to go out, how no one understands him, and that he lives in a black space that only he occupies. By 'relating' to her he starts building a rapport, gaining her trust, making her feel that he understands her and is on her side. He keeps answering her post until eventually they start conversing more frequently.

Paedophiles do not use a real picture of themselves in their profile. The beauty of the Internet is that you can invent a profile – you can hide behind any façade you have constructed and want the world to see you as. You live vicariously through the persona you have invented. Then the conversations start becoming too long and personal to have on Facebook, so he asks her to rather move to a chat room, a space where they can converse away from 'other people'. He gives her a nickname. He only calls her this name – it is their secret, their special word. They exchange pictures of thin people and perhaps make fun of others, repeatedly enforcing the 'bond' between them. Soon he has her phone number and their interaction progresses to texting as messages are received immediately without her having to be online. Before long, the phone calls become a normal part of her day. He has seen her pictures posted on her site, blog or profile, and started to get more personal with her. He says nice things about her, telling her that she is beautiful and very appealing. He might ask her to send him photos of herself that are not on the web, but only for him. She feels flattered. She depends on this communication in a world where no one understands her, except him. He cares. He phones her to see how she is. He is concerned about her. He thinks about her. She is important to him.

Then they move to the next level, where he will ask her not to be angry because he is a lot older than he has made himself out to be. This disclosure is crucial because through it he can gauge her reaction and whether the relationship can progress to the next level, the level of using webcams and exchanging more intimate photos. She forgives him because she 'understands' that other people will not understand the special connection they have. She might even feel very flattered that an older person is interested in her. This makes her feel more mature, more grown up. She feels elevated above her friends. She has joined the world of adults and it's all been on her terms. He starts to send her pictures of himself, more and more pictures. Then he sends pictures of himself with no shirt. He goads her into taking photos of her body. It can start off with "a pic of my butt", and progress to something more intimate. If a webcam is involved, conversing in real time is a bonus – she feels as if he is there with her. This progresses to more risky behaviour, which involves taking off her clothes and then, later, being asked to touch herself. All the while she is being praised, encouraged and goaded by the paedophile. This exchange entrenches the 'our secret'; it entrenches behaviour that can, and sometimes is, used against her. He will be recording her taking off her clothes, touching herself, talking dirty, repeating words and phrases he wants to hear. He has leverage over her – he can blackmail her with these pictures and videos if he needs to; he can threaten to flood Facebook with these images under a fake profile that he has invented. If, on the other hand, she shows a willingness to continue the relationship, he may arrange to meet her. Stories of young females meeting older men on the Internet and meeting up with them in a hotel room, only to be raped, are not unusual.

Understanding the lingo

It is quite likely that your child will be using what is commonly referred to as 'txt talk' or 'chatspeak'. This is an abbreviated, shorthand language used to send text and instant messages. It enables quick and efficient communication, but could also be used by your child to hide the real meaning behind their messages. Here is a list of the most important abbreviations that you should know.

AFK / BAK	Away from keyboard / Back at keyboard
121	One-to-one
ASL?	Age, sex, location?
PA	Parent alert
PAL	Parents are listening
POS	Parents over shoulder
P911	Parent alert
NIFOC	Naked in front of computer
MorF	Male or female
SorG	Straight or gay
LMIRL	Let's meet in real life
TDTM	Talk dirty to me
ADR	Address
WYCM?	Will you call me?
F2F	Face to face
WRN?	What's your real name?
WUF?	Where are you from?
53x	Sex
Cyber	Cybersex, sex over the computer
WTGP	Want to go private?

Cyber bullying

Cyber bullying involves the use of websites, text messages, emails and social forums to harm, harass, threaten, discredit, control, manipulate, tease or humiliate other people. At the time of publication, according to the Centre for Disease Control, 25% of cyber bullying occurs in chat rooms, 23% on websites, a whopping 67% in instant messaging, 25% in emails, and 16% in text messaging.

The victim

When someone says nasty things, mentally and emotionally secure people can filter those things out – they're able to put a block between what's being said and what they know to be true. But mentally and/or emotionally insecure people don't have the strength or self-esteem to do that – to them, what is said becomes the absolute truth; there's no filter, no block. They take the information to heart and it slowly starts eroding their world and whatever is left of their fragile self-esteem. They may become depressed and feel hopeless – for some victims, suicide seems like the only option out of the nightmare in which they find themselves living.

Everyday youngsters are bombarded with sexually suggestive and explicit images by the media of how they must look and behave. They're fed a cornucopia of movies and programmes such as Paris Hilton, Keeping up with the Kardashians, Toddlers and Tiaras, to name but a few. These programmes feature intimate portrayals of famous peoples' lives – lives that revolve around money and being noticed. We live in an age where a 'Like' button on Facebook has more bearing on your social status and how you feel than having privileges revoked when you dare to defy your parent's instructions not to do the very things the media is encouraging you to do. Teenagers are particularly vulnerable as they are in that fragile period of their lives where they seek constant affirmation for their looks and behavior. Affirmation is given in abundance on blogs and sites such as Facebook and Twitter. By the same token, a 'Dislike' button on these very same sites can have devastating effects on youngsters. One of the most damaging effects of cyber bullying is that a victim begins to avoid friends and activities, often the very intention of the cyber bully. Unfortunately, cyber bullying can also lead to more fatal outcomes such as when young people take their lives in response to taunts being made on Facebook or repeated harassment or humiliation online or via text messaging.

The cyber bully

A cyber bully may be a person whom the target knows or it could be an online stranger. A cyber bully may solicit involvement of other people online who do not even know the target. This is known as a 'digital pile-on'. Cyber bullying by proxy is when the bully gets someone else to do the dirty work for them.

When cyber bullying is directed at adults, the bullying is usually referred to as cyber stalking or cyber harassment.

Here, the crime is aimed more at attacking the person's status in society, their earnings, safety, reputation, identity, spreading rumours, and gathering information that can later be used to threaten the victim.

A cyber bully is different to a troll in that cyber bullies want to hurt you; a troll wants to incite you – make you mad. Trolls make inflammatory or ridiculous comments on public online forums to get an amusing or angry reaction from the people on those forums. A site like REDDIT is a classic example of a social forum that works by posting a topic and getting as many people as possible to vote for it or submit a comment in return. Unfortunately, it also attracts trolls. The overwhelming majority of trolls leave after a few minutes of trolling, especially when they're ignored.

A cyber bully, on the other hand, targets a specific person with the deliberate intention of hurting or humiliating them, and feeds off their victim's reaction as a bonus. A cyber bully does things on the Internet that they would not or can't do face to face. Cyber bullies continue to bully over a prolonged period.

So why do cyber bullies do what they do? Well, for one, they benefit from the lack of face-to-face interaction on the Web, which allows them to do or say outrageous things that would normally have serious consequences if said in the real world. They can bully someone bigger than them or someone they are intimidated by. Verbal abuse is very eroding, sometimes more so than physical abuse, and difficult to prove in a court of law. For people who are relatively isolated and feel powerless in their ordinary lives – the Net provides a world where they can wield power, gather 'Likes' on social networking sites, and influence others.

Cyber bullies do what they do for different reasons.

- Sometimes it can be to 'right a wrong', for instance, they or someone they know is physically bullied in real life so they use an online platform to get back at the person bullying them, or they may be trying to teach the other person a lesson for something they believe that person did wrong. These types of bullies often work alone but may share their activities with close friends or those they perceive as having been victimised by the person they are bullying.
- Sometimes they want to exert their authority, show that they are powerful enough to make others do what they want or to control others. These bullies like an audience – it may be a small audience of friends at school. They often brag about their actions and want a reaction. If they don't get one, they may escalate their activities until they do.
- Sometimes they are simply bored and looking for entertainment. This type of bullying requires an audience and usually grows when fed by group admiration and participation – it may also be planned in a group. The bully wants others to know who they are and that they have the power to bully others. This type of bullying also dies quickly if the bully doesn't get the entertainment value they are seeking.

- Sometimes they just lash out without thinking about the consequences. They may feel hurt or angry about a communication sent to them and retaliate out of anger or frustration. Their actions tend to be impulsive as opposed to those of the cyber bully who is trying to deliberately right a wrong. This last type of bully may also be playing a joke on someone they know, not thinking about the seriousness of what they're doing. They do it just because they can.

Top sites for bullying are Myspace, Facebook and Reddit.

Examples of direct attacks include:
- Hateful, derogatory or critical messages posted on blogs
- Stealing passwords for instant messages and emails
- Websites that are created to tease and hurt
- Pictures sent via the Internet
- Internet polling e.g. who is hot, who is not
- Sending porn, superimposing a person's face on a naked body
- Sending harmful computer viruses, spam, junk mail
- Interactive gaming e.g. X-Box live, Sony PlayStation
- Harassment through text, instant messaging and email
- Impersonating another person.

Useful Internet sites for parents

As a parent, your primary concern will be to keep your kids happy, healthy and safe online. This involves educating both yourself and your children about the Internet and digital media.

Here are some excellent resources and child-friendly media sites you might find very helpful:

www.safety.aol.com

www.ciconline.org/media-smart

www.commonsensemedia.org

www.cyberangels.org

www.ikeepsafe.org

www.isafe.org

www.pointsmartclicksafe.org

www.staysafeonline.org

www.netsmartz.org

www.puresight.com

www.meganmeierfoundation.org

www.stopcyberbullying.org

www.parentfurther.com/high-risk-behaviors/bullying/
cyberbullying

http://www.parents.com/kids/problems/bullying/18-tips-
to-stop-cyberbullying

www.cyberbullyhelp.com

www.cybersafetysolutions.com.au

www.netalert.gov.au

www.netsafe.org.nz

www.ceop.gov.uk

www.CyberTipline.org

www.bullying.org

www.wiredsafety.org

www.GetNetWise.org

www.kidshelpline.com.au

www.dosomething.org/tipsandtools/11-facts-about-cyber-
bullying
www.nathantimothyfoundation.org
https://familyshare.com/22280/child-grooming-the-new-
danger-on-the-net
http://www.oprah.com/oprahshow/child-sexual-abuse-6-
stages-of-grooming/all
http://www.sdcda.org/preventing/protecting-children-
online/facts-for-parents.html

Internet packages to help parents monitor Internet usage

www.internet-filter-review.toptenreviews.com
www1.k9webprotection.com

Sites to watch out for and be careful of

Violent porn sites e.g. hogtide.com
Youtube
Video chat rooms
Pro anorexia sites
Pro cutting sites
Addictive games
Violent games
Hate groups
Miss bimbo

Help in the media and pop culture

- Adina's Deck – a film about three 8th-graders who help their friend who's been cyber bullied.
- Let's Fight It Together – a film produced by Childnet International for use in schools to support discussion and awareness-raising around cyber bullying.
- Odd Girl Out – a film about a girl who is bullied at school and online.
- At a Distance – a short film produced by NetSafe for the 8 to 12-year-old audience helping them to stand up to bullying
- Cyber bully – a TV movie broadcast on ABC Family; similar to Odd Girl Out, it also depicts a girl who is bullied at school and online.
- The Casual Vacancy – a young girl is subjected to harassing images repeatedly posted on her Facebook page.
- The Truth about Truman School – a 2008 children's book about a middle school girl who is cyber bullied by one of her classmates.

CHAPTER 5

Attending to the problem

So how do we attend to the problem of child sexual abuse? Since I've already mentioned that intrafamilial abuse is the most common form of child sexual abuse, let's begin there.

What about the young girl who is being abused by her father and cannot tell her mother? Most children who come to the clinic say that the father has threatened them in some way or told them that their mother won't believe them.

Let's consider the child who *has* told her mother and nothing has been done. There could be many reasons for this.

1. The father is the breadwinner. The mother realises that by laying a charge he could possibly go to jail; she can't afford to lose the breadwinner as she and her family are dependent on him. How would they survive, where would they go?

2. The mother was sexually abused herself and cannot deal with this. She is catapulted back into the victim phase of her life and shuts herself off from her daughter, thus remaining in victim mode.

3. The mother is frigid and only too happy to allow that function to be filled by her daughter. Yes, this is true, it happens!

4. The mother feels too weak or afraid to take the matter further, particularly if she's the victim of regular abuse; she may fear for her own life and the life of her abused child if she says or does anything to challenge the father.

5. The mother refuses to believe that her husband – or partner – is capable of such a thing; she takes his side over the child's in an act of denial.

4. In some cultures, such as the Indian community, it is not unusual for the extended family to be living together under one roof. Should the mother lay a charge, she will have to face the rest of the family – the aunts and uncles, and grandparents. She will undergo secondary abuse for the 'look what you've done' syndrome; she is afraid of the shame it will bring on her family so she is forced, in a way, to silently collude with the father. This is not hard to understand in a world where, in the twenty-first century, we are still fighting archaic issues such as women being stoned to death for having a child out of wedlock; husbands 'owning' their wives in certain cultures and therefore having the right to beat and rape

them; infibulation. The list is endless. Iraq passed a law in 2014 that girls as young as eight years old can be married! Through socialisation women have become the possessions of men; in patriarchal systems, this becomes entrenched.

As a paramedic who has worked on the road for more than fourteen years, I have seen the attitudes of policemen who arrive at a domestic dispute. It's obvious they don't want to go there in the first place, and they don't treat it as a serious issue. There is still the belief that the man is the head of the house and in his house, he is king. If, however, it is public domestic abuse, then it seems to spur them on to do something because there are too many witnesses. How many times have you read a story about a woman who went to the police station having been threatened, and terrified that her husband might kill her? She's normally told that there's nothing they can do until a crime has been committed, and when he eventually does kill her, it's too late. Most abused women are abused by their spouses or partners, not by strangers. It's the same story with children; most are abused by someone they know.

So, back to attending to the problem.

Well, let's see ... you could go out and beat the perpetrator to a pulp, but it's not going to help your child if you end up in prison. Besides, your child needs you, not your anger. You could hurt the abuser where it hurts most, by boycotting his business – if he has one. You could phone him at all hours of the night but that means you won't get any sleep either. You could move your child to another school, if that's where the problem lies, but I strongly advise against this as it sends the wrong message to the child; it tells the child you are hiding her, you are embarrassed to keep her where she is. And the perpetrator would still be at large and able to abuse other children at that school. You could also confront him and say: "We all know what you have done, we are all watching you," and leave it at that and let him worry himself into insanity.

There's no denying that this is a difficult area, especially when it is a family member. I have watched countless parents in my group in tears as it rips families apart, with the mother undergoing secondary abuse because she laid a charge against the husband. I have often seen families begin the court process and give up because of intimidation, bribes, and other means of getting them to back off. Please remember that once a charge has been laid, it cannot be retracted by the parents; the child is a ward of the state and it is being done in the best interests of the child. This is a reality that the family must live with, so there is no true right or wrong thing to do, but I can give you some guidelines.

What to do when a child tells

Hearing that your child has been abused has got to be the hardest thing for a parent to hear, more especially if you hear it from the child itself. You will feel like imploding as a range of emotions runs through you in seconds. It's very hard to maintain composure, but you must for the child's sake. If you lose control, the child will clam up and it will reinforce in their mind that they shouldn't have come to tell you. Remember, the child needs your attention, your time, your understanding – not your anger. This is not about you. Take a deep breath. Hug them tight as you gather yourself together.

Be mindful that when a child comes to tell you, it is not an easy thing for them to do. They feel ashamed, they feel dirty, they feel guilty, and they feel they won't be believed, so to get to the point where they eventually come out with it, you must appreciate that it was very difficult for them to do so. It probably involved many sleepless nights and enormous courage.

- Firstly, remember when speaking to them that they have been intimidated to a point, so make good eye contact and come down to their level. Give your full, undivided attention. Don't interrupt, and don't fire off questions like a machine gun. Do not answer your phone if it rings.

- Don't react in horror, disgust, outrage or anger. Remember, the abuser may be a person that they love, like their father. They don't love the behaviour, but they may love the person.

- Be patient with them, don't butt in; let them finish their sentences and say what they are trying to express. Remember that a small child's natural form of communication is playing, not talking. Respect their silence no matter how difficult it is. Ensure that they know you are there for them, this will usually spur them on to tell you more.

- Remind them that, while they are with you in that room, they are safe. You cannot always guarantee their safety, so verbalise "in this room, right now, you are safe with me".

- Don't promise the child anything you personally cannot carry out. For instance, don't tell the child you will put a stop to this if you don't have that power – you will be yet another adult who lies to them and betrays them.

- Make it clear that you believe them. Remember that children lie to get *out* of trouble, not into it. There are incidents of children lying, but these are usually older children where one parent may tutor the child to say something against the other, as in a custody case. These are the exceptions, not the norm.

- Tell the child you are proud of them, and acknowledge their bravery. Use sentences like, "I know it was not easy for you to tell", "I want you to know how brave you are", "You did the right thing to tell me".

- Tell them that what happened to them is not their fault; they are not to blame. Use sentences like, "I want you to know that this is not your fault", "You have done nothing wrong", "It is not because of who you are that this bad thing happened to you".

- Don't touch the child unnecessarily – be mindful of how you touch them. Don't grab them and place them on your knee.

- Be very clear that, to be able to help them, and with their permission, you are going to have to tell another adult. You can say, "What you are telling me is very important, so I want to write it down. Is that okay? Can I do that?" Do NOT substitute their words for yours – this is very important from a legal point of view; use *their* words no matter how strange they might be, or how disjointed the story sounds. Write everything down word for word.

- Remind them that they can always talk to you; it's reassuring for them to open up. Initially they might not have told you verbally so you should approach them with caution. It is acceptable to say things like, "I've noticed that you haven't been yourself lately, you can come and talk to me whenever you want to." Reinforce this because it's important. Children don't always answer well to direct questions. Research shows that one of the first requirements for a disclosure to take place is a safe space. If the child feels safe in that space, they're more likely to disclose.[11]

- Don't ask accusing questions like "Did your father give you that bruise?"

---

[11] (Paine, M., Hansen, D., 2002, Factors influencing children to self disclose sexual abuse, Clinical Psychology Review, Volume 22, pages 271–295).

- Remind them it was not their fault; it is always the adult's fault.

Very often a child will tell another child first. This is very difficult for a parent to accept, but you mustn't take it personally. I saw parents in my group struggle with this. Try to remember that the child has been told it's her fault; she was the seducer, and so on. She is ashamed, she is scared, she fears that she will not be believed. As the law now stands, the first person who was told of the abuse is the one who gives testimony in Court, apart from the victim. Everything after that is considered hearsay evidence. So, make sure the child knows it was the right thing to do to come and tell you, as hard as this is. Thank them for telling you. Tell them that you are sorry this has happened to them, and that you believe them, and that you will try to make it right. Explain that in doing that, it will involve telling a policeman/woman and that you will always be with them. Reinforce that you will be doing everything with them, each step of the way. If you cannot stop yourself from crying, explain that you are sad this has happened to them and that you are sorry you were not there to stop it, but you are here now. Remind them that you love them; remember, they very often feel worthless, not good enough, soiled.

If the child is in immediate danger, for example they are bleeding profusely, take them to a casualty straight away, or call for an ambulance. Do not remove the clothes they're wearing – keep them as evidence, and do not bathe the child. It's okay for the child to urinate; this will not damage any evidence. Explain that she will need to be examined but that you will be with her all the time. This is all so much easier said than done because at this moment in time you are not thinking rationally. But remember, your child needs your support, not your anger or uncontrolled emotion.

Decide what you are going to do about this tragic event and stick to it. Unfortunately, there is no straightforward black-and-white answer.

Document everything. Get the contact details of your investigating officer. It is up to you to phone and keep abreast of the case; do not rely on the police calling you – they are dealing with hundreds of other cases and are usually snowed under. This is your child; following up is your responsibility. If you are going to the hospital, take a fresh set of loose clothing and nice-smelling bath stuff for after the examination; your child may be feeling dirty and ugly. Also bring along a favourite toy. Be with your child.

Be sure that if you want to take the legal route you must stick to it and follow it through. I will not sugar-coat this – it is hard, it rips families apart, you feel as if you're going insane, nothing makes sense. You might feel ashamed, and you can become numb and start to fall apart yourself. Don't expect to cope with it in the beginning – nothing prepares you for something like this. Make sure you have a support structure of some kind – a best friend, a family member. You also need to take time out for yourself; engage in something that is nurturing and provides you with 'soul' food. Be gentle and kind on yourself – look after yourself.

In terms of support, I must add here that I have also seen, countless times, parents who are part of a church group turning to the group for support. The group pressurises the mother to drop the charges and pray for the perpetrator, instead. Perpetrators need punishment! The perpetrator, like any other person who commits a crime, needs to be held accountable for his actions. He needs to take responsibility for what he has done and for the irreparable pain and damage that he has caused. **Most importantly, the perpetrator must be taken off the streets so that other children can be protected!**

Also give a thought to women who, by virtue of their culture, are not recognised as even remotely close to being equal to men; women who live in countries like Saudi Arabia – imagine what it must be like for such a mother to hear that she must take legal action. They don't have the basic luxury of freedom to go to a police station, for instance. She is dependent on her husband to do this.

Do not underestimate the power of your support for your child. It has a wonderful healing power of its own. You won't be able to see it when it's happening, but when that child is much older, they'll look back and say; "My Mom/ Dad believed me, they went through hell and back, but they stood by me."

I'll never forget a parent in my group who had four daughters. The two oldest ones came to tell her that their father was abusing them and she ignored them for years. Eventually they both ran away from home. I remember her words:

"Every night I would lock the doors to keep the monsters out – meanwhile the monster was lying right next to me in bed." When the two younger daughters came to tell her the same story, she finally believed them. She suffered the worst kind of regret at not having believed her oldest two, with whom she still has no contact. She cried when telling the group the story, and it took ages for all that pain to come out. She was a shell of a woman; guilt and regret are two terrible companions to live with. My heart broke for her, watching her raw emotions being exposed in front of a room full of strangers. Like an emotional volcano, she was finally able to release all that incredible shame and pain.

What about fathers? In a society where men are supposed to be tough, where boys are told to "go back on the rugby field and finish the game, never mind the broken collar bone", what should they do? Women generally turn anger inwards, and learn to deal with it that way, but men turn anger outwards and tend to strike out – they want to hit someone, to kick things.

After and during the process of taking the child to court, it is important for you as a father to show them that you, too, feel anger. *However, it's vital to show them how to channel that anger properly!* Get a punching bag, a squash racquet and ball, rip up newspapers … explain to your child that when you feel angry, empty, frustrated or low, this is what you do. If the victim is your son, use the punching bag together; remind him that it's normal to feel all those emotions and that you're there for him. It is not okay to shut off, go drinking, or take it out on the rest of the family. Remind him that it's not okay for him to take it out on another person either, particularly his siblings. Make it clear that to hurt another person will not solve anything, it will exacerbate the problem.

As a parent, you need to be consistent in your behaviour towards your child and keep things as normal as possible. This means:

- Do not single them out from the rest of the family and stop them from doing what you always did as a family. For instance, if dinner is normally at 6pm, then stick to 6pm – don't allow the child to change the rules.

- Do not take them out of school if it happened at the school; this sends a message that you *don't* want to deliver, namely, that they are to blame, or that you are so embarrassed that you can't handle the situation. It may reinforce feelings of shame in the child.

- Do take the child's teacher aside and tell him/her briefly what has happened so that he/she will understand a possible change in behaviour. Ask particularly that the child not be singled out and not be allowed any special privileges. They should be treated the same as the other children.

- If it happened at school, go to the headmaster and explain what has happened, and that you are taking legal action against the perpetrator. Ask what the headmaster or headmistress is going to do about it. When I was a counsellor at Childline, I came across a case where the headmaster of a prominent school wouldn't pursue the matter for fear of the damaging publicity the school would receive. This is like the Roman Catholic Church 'dealing with the matter internally'.

- If you are taking the legal route, *do not* get the child to discuss the event with you, as this can be very damaging to the case. When the child testifies in court, they might use words you've used, and when they are being cross-examined, the defence might ask them what that word means. If they're unable to explain, it can make the testimony look like a slice of Emmentaler cheese – full of holes. If the child discloses something, contact the prosecutor and the investigating officer so that it can be entered into the testimony.

- Remind the child how beautiful and special they are, how sorry you are about what happened and that you are there for them.

- If the family and/or friends of the perpetrator start to intimidate you or try to bribe you, you need to let the officer working on your case know so that more restrictions are placed on his/her bail. This is discussed in more detail in the next chapter.

- Do not berate the child if she/he told someone else first. This will only compound the feelings of guilt the child already has. Remember, children do not want to burden you with this information – they want your approval and for the family to be okay – so they will often tell someone else. Don't take this personally.

Important medical matters

If you wish to lay a charge, your child should *preferably* be taken to a Clinical Medico-Legal Service (previously called the District Surgeon) or a place where the *correct* examination can be made, such as a rape-crisis unit. Most private hospitals, particularly Netcare, have a rape-crisis unit in their casualties, where the doctors and nurses are trained to fill out the correct forms and complete the rape kit. You can also try ER24 or any of the Life Hospitals. Alternatively, you can phone your local SAP and ask to be connected to the Victim Empowerment Officer or Centre, then ask for the contact details of the cluster Family, Child and Sexual Offences Unit, or you can call Childline and ask for your nearest rape-crisis unit or Clinical Medico-Legal Service.

The medical examiners will fill in a J88 form, which is the forensic medical examination form. If you *suspect* that your child has been molested, you should, instead, take your child to an assessment centre, such as the Teddy Bear Clinic in Johannesburg or the Tygerbear Clinic in Cape Town (or call Childline for an assessment centre near you). The assessment centre will perform a full assessment and/or examination. You may be present when the child is being examined. The Teddy Bear Clinic has paediatricians who do examinations on certain days, during office hours.

Most local general practitioners are not specifically trained in this area and may not know how to examine sexually-abused victims. They might just write a script for a vaginal infection without further investigation. If you use a general practitioner, be sure to ask about Post-Exposure Prophylaxis for HIV, STIs and, if appropriate, pregnancy – this is essential within the first 72 hours after a sexual assault.

Doctors need to complete a Sexual Assault Evidence Collection Kit (SAECK), commonly known as a rape kit, to collect forensic evidence if semen is present, or if you take the child for examination within the first 72 hours after the assault.

To compile the SAECK, the medical examiner completes various forms; takes swabs to form a DNA baseline; collects pubic hair; and draws blood samples to check for STDs and HIV, and for DNA identification. The SAECK is a sealed unit and is fetched by the police directly from the casualty or the medical examiner; the complainant or any member of their family may not take it to the police station – this obviates the possibility of tampering with evidence or disrupting the chain of evidence.

The SAECK is the medical evidence that is usually brought before a court. Deposits of semen in the rectum and/or vagina, and tear marks that are fresh or in certain stages of healing, are factors that make the evidence compelling; these fall into the 'more than suggestive of' category. In certain age groups where consent is not in question, this would be considered conclusive evidence. I cannot emphasise this enough: if your child was sexually assaulted, have them examined. **If you want to stack the odds for a conviction, you need to follow the correct procedures right from the**

beginning. Medical evidence is always relevant, even if there are no injuries. The doctor can come forward and give reasons why there are no obvious injuries. For example, in the case of an adult examination, the complainant could have given birth recently or the complainant could have been drugged or drunk and her body was relaxed during the rape.

What a teacher can do[12]

You are in the unique position of possibly spending more time with a child than the child's parents do. If you are fortunate enough to be a Waldorf or Montessori teacher where the classes are very small, you will be able to pick up a behavioural change in a child fairly quickly. A teacher who must keep an eye on many children might miss the signs in the beginning.

By law

Many teachers and educators are completely unaware of the law regarding the policy of dealing with the sexual abuse of a child; be it by a parent, a sibling, or perhaps another child or teacher at the school. Many people in authority are unaware that *the law compels them to report cases of suspected*

---

[12] To read the letter of the law (Section 110 of the amended Children's Act (41 of 2007)) and for further discussion on reporting suspected abuse, see page 67.

abuse. Possibly this could be attributed to the fact that there is no formal document available to teachers. However, an excellent manual was written in 2008, which was an initiative between the Teddy Bear Clinic and the Gauteng Department of Education, compiled by Luke Lampbrecht, Anthony Wild and Tina Labuschagne.

Teachers also seem to collude because they don't want to tell the principal and be the one who 'rocked the boat'. What would happen if the principal is abusing the child?

In cases that are reported to the principal, it is the *responsibility of the school* to follow up with the family. If the family has stated that they will report the abuse to the police, the school must be given the case number within ten days. This is obligatory under section 1.4.

Bear in mind that you are reporting the matter because it is in the best interests of the child; and because you are operating from this platform, you cannot be sued – unless you are reckless enough to point fingers directly at someone or name someone when you do not know the facts. You need to report suspected abuse when it seems that the child is in immediate danger, needs assistance because you have seen obvious marks on the child, or the child has been brave enough to come to you and disclose.

Teachers are not allowed to remove the child from the school without a parent's permission, unless the child requires immediate medical intervention or is in immediate danger and reasonable attempts to contact the parents have failed.

QUICK EMERGENCY CHECKLIST
What to do if your child has been abused

WHEN YOU FIND OUT

- Offer your support. Let your child know that you believe them and you will be with them each step of the way. Reassure them that it's not their fault – it's not because of who they are that this happened; the adult who did this to them is wrong.
- Let them know that their story is very important and you don't want to miss anything out, so you need to write everything down, if that's okay. Gently ask them to tell you the whole story and let them know that it's okay if they cry. Use the exact words the child uses; do not replace words or paraphrase. Do not 'help them out' by giving them the words if they can't find the words themselves. This is very important from a legal perspective. Be patient.
- When the child has finished telling you, thank them. Let them know how brave they were to have told you, that you believe them, and that you are sorry you weren't able to stop it. Reaffirm how special and beautiful they are, and ask them if you can give them a hug. Remind them that they are not to blame.
- Tell them that if they want to stop the abuse, you are going to have to tell another adult, like a policeman. Reassure them that you will be with them all the time; they will not be alone.

- The child must understand that if you report the abuse, the perpetrator may be angry with them and threaten them; remind the child again that they are not in the wrong – the person who did this to them is wrong.
- At no point should you show, in front of the child, your anger or disgust towards the perpetrator; this moment is not about you. Remember: most abuse is perpetrated by someone the child knows and probably loves – they cannot separate the person and the deed.

IF YOU WANT TO LAY A CHARGE

- First, take the child to the police station to lay a charge – remind the child that they are safe and you will remain with them.
- Make it clear from the beginning that it is not a fair process; the abuser might get off and not be punished. What is important is that the child gets to tell their story, a very important story.
- If the abuse has just happened, the child must not shower or bath, as forensic evidence will need to be taken (it's safe to urinate). Evidence can be taken up to 72 hours after the rape or abuse has taken place. Take the child's clothing with you for DNA evidence if the child is not still wearing it.

- The child should be medically examined, preferably at a rape-crisis unit or by a Clinical Medico-Legal Service. Explain to the child that blood will need to be taken and their body is going to be photographed, but you will be there with them all the time.
- If the child requires immediate medical attention, take them to the hospital casualty first – the hospital staff will notify the police; check that this is done.
- Bring a bag of your child's clothes with you – preferably loose – plus something to snack on and a favourite toy or two; also bring nice-smelling bath goodies for after the examination – your child may be feeling dirty and ugly.
- Follow up with the police regarding the case – do not expect them to call you.
- Keep things at home and at school as normal as possible – do not change your routine or give special privileges to your child; your child needs to feel normal, like everyone else.
- Join a support group, and remember to look after yourself, too.

Childline – 08000 55555

Call Childline for information on your nearest Violence and Sexual Assault Unit or hospital with a rape crisis unit – or for general child-abuse support and guidance.

CHAPTER 6

The legal route

In our country, we have an accusatory system that has been in existence since Roman times. That means that one person accuses another person of committing a crime. The accuser is known as the *plaintiff* or *complainant*. The perpetrator is called the *accused* only after being charged. There is no jury system in our country. The magistrate passes sentence on the evidence brought before him from both the prosecuting side (lawyers for the complainant) and from the defence (lawyers for the accused). The accused is assumed to be innocent until proven guilty. The rape of children is a schedule-six offence, as is murder, armed robbery and vehicle hijacking; all these offences carry possible life sentences.

Officers of the court

The important officers in a High Court Division are:

- The *Registrar* keeps all the official court documents
- The *Family Advocate* must be consulted on all matters involving children, as the High Court is the 'upper guardian' of all children in South Africa
- The *Master of the High Court* keeps all the records relating to people's estates (deceased or insolvent)
- The *Sheriff* delivers certain documents to the parties in a civil case, and attaches property when a warrant is issued
- The *Director of Public Prosecutions*, who used to be called the *Attorney-General*, is responsible for criminal prosecutions by the State
- The *State Attorney* is the lawyer who represents the State in civil actions (where the State is suing or being sued)

After the arrest

Within 48 hours of being arrested the accused is brought before a magistrate and his rights are explained to him/her. For example, his right to legal representation, or his right to bring a formal bail application where bail has been opposed. If the arresting officer is aware of any history of previous crimes of a similar nature, he can oppose bail. Bail can now be refused when an offence has caused community outrage; however, the Bill makes it clear that this will only be in exceptional circumstances.

Bail is an absolute right throughout most of the world. It has nothing to do with whether the accused is guilty or not; at this stage, he is assumed innocent until proven guilty. The person being charged receives his bail money back only if he is found 'not guilty.' If he doesn't have a fixed address or any form of identification, he is viewed as a flight risk, and this can be a factor in the bail dispensation.

It is important to remember that in our country, the police have limited resources. This is not America where they have a VICAP system where information is punched into a computer that is linked nationally, and immediately spews out information on previous convictions. This is unfortunately also not CSI where you scan a fingerprint in minutes and get a match in seconds. The police are overworked and greatly underpaid. Each detective has more than 20 cases at any given time. In Britain, the system is the other way around – you can have up to four detectives working on one case, which makes them seem more efficient than we are. Under the Criminal Procedure Amendment Bill, South Africa does have a national computer system where limited information can be checked.

The first time anyone is asked to appear in court, they are served with a written document called a *subpoena*. He or she will appear and the next court date will be decided upon. This will be stated verbally, and is not sent again in *subpoena* form. It is up to you, the parent, to phone your arresting officer to follow up and find out when the next court date is. You must realise that the police are dealing with many ongoing matters all the time, so the responsibility for your individual case becomes yours. If you don't hear when the next date is, I suggest that you follow up yourself. This is your child and your lives that are being turned upside down.

You need to minimise the stress by being empowered. Disempowered people usually operate from a position of assumptions and guesses. Know the facts! I have explained that the detective will usually be dealing with twenty or more cases at any one time. They also are out 'in the field' gathering evidence, not sitting at their desks, and cannot always get back to you. If you are unhappy with your arresting officer, there is a procedure to follow. Phone the station commander and tell him your concern. There is a police hierarchy and the correct procedure must be followed.

Write down in your diary all the relevant information and dates. You must know the court dates when you are required to appear; you must know the case number and the contact numbers of your arresting officer. If you do not appear in court when you are supposed to, that is called contempt of court. In other words, you have transgressed an order made by the court and you could be fined.

The trial

The prosecuting side presents their case first. The onus is on the State to prove guilt – it is not on the defence to prove innocence. Then, the defence may cross-question the victim.

The onus is weighted heavily on the prosecuting team; they must prove that this person committed the crime, beyond a reasonable doubt. That involves bringing before the court proof in the form of statements and written, medical and oral evidence.

If the accused has been previously accused of a similar crime, or successfully convicted, these cases may not be brought to the attention of the court during the trial because they are viewed as separate crimes. This is set out by the specific Criminal Procedure Act (CPA) and Act 108/1996, and has nothing to do with the current case being presented before the court. This sometimes feels very unfair to the complainant, because they may feel it has relevance, but it's all about human rights. How many American TV series have we seen that ended most unsatisfactorily because of this fact of law?

Sexual abuse of children carries the maximum sentence of life (25 years). To impose such a sentence, the magistrate must be presented with overwhelming evidence that is beyond any reasonable doubt (Act 32/2007). And even then, it doesn't always mean that the accused will receive a life sentence. His age, previous convictions, and other factors need to be considered by the magistrate before passing sentence, according to the minimum sentencing act. The National Prosecuting Authority in South Africa has released a document that makes for very interesting reading: Final Report – Review, Research and Evaluation of the 'Ke Bona Lesedi' Draft Court Preparation Programme of the National Prosecution Authority, 2008.

The onus on the defence is not as difficult as that on the prosecution. The defence must prove that their client did not commit this crime, by asking the victim many questions. The defence must also discredit the witnesses that the prosecution puts on the stand, showing their testimony to be unstable, conflicting, vascilating. The prosecution's job is to find inconsistencies in the statements, casting doubt on the so-called evidence of innocence.

All children under eighteen may suffer undue mental stress if they testify in front of the accused. For this reason, they will testify in a special court room – this is a room where an intermediary, appointed at the court's discretion, will be sitting with the child. The intermediary will wear headphones that are linked to the main courtroom. They listen to the question and repeat it to the child one-on-one in a child-friendly manner. The courtroom has a TV monitor linked to it, so the answer is seen and heard. The use of this special courtroom is at the discretion of the prosecutor and/or magistrate (or judge if the case is held in the Supreme Court). This is not an absolute rule yet, as not all cities in our country have them. Children over eighteen usually testify in the main courtroom.

After the defence has cross-questioned the victim, the prosecutor may re-question the victim to confirm any comments or statements that might seem inconsistent or be detrimental to their case.

The magistrate passes sentence on the facts brought before the court.

An acquittal means the prosecuting side could not prove the accused guilty of committing the crime beyond reasonable doubt. Acquitted doesn't mean the accused is not guilty – it means there was insufficient evidence.

Evidence

Written evidence is provided in the form of a statement submitted by the victim. It can include reports from teachers, social workers, play therapists and psychologists. The victim may read his or her statement again before he/she goes into court, in case something new is suddenly remembered.

Oral evidence is the testimony given in court by the victim.

Medical evidence is normally only supplementary. It is only brought before the court when there is a need to prove that a case was "more than suggestive of...". For instance, a child who has been anally raped over a long period of time, could show poor anal tone and scarring on the tissue inside the rectum. This could be indicative of abuse.

CHAPTER 7

Preparing children for court

The children are divided into age groups – the youngest ones, the four to six-year-olds in one group, teenagers in another group, and so on. Various techniques are used, depending on the age of the child. The prep course normally takes about three hours. This is a very long time for the little ones, and I really have to admire the counsellors who work with them. During the process of preparing them, we never use words like 'we 'or 'them' or even refer to the perpetrator as 'the bad one'; we are careful not to put words in their mouths. We try our utmost to prepare a child for court at their language level.

With the young ones, it is important to establish if they can differentiate between the truth and a lie. If it is observed that the child cannot tell the difference, the clinic advises the prosecutor to hold the case back and take it temporarily off the court roll. With these little ones, a technique called the 'worry cup' is then used in the preparation. The child is presented with three different sized cups – small, medium and large. The child is asked: "What things concern you about going to court? What makes you worried?" When the child verbalises the worry, it is written down on a piece of paper and placed in the big worry cup. That morning, the child will be taught about going to court. We tell them that they are going to tell their story. Counsellors use puppets and other methods to help them understand what will happen. A centre such as the Teddy Bear Clinic is fortunate to have a room that is a replica of a real court room. It is all made of wood, and the older kids get to role play in costumes as lawyers, judges and various other officials. If at any stage during the preparation for court, a child discloses something about the case, the counsellor makes sure it is reported to the relevant authorities.

At the close of the process, the child is asked to take out the piece of paper from the big worry cup and to read the worry out loud. The counsellor has taught them during that morning that it is okay to cry, it is okay to want to go to the toilet, and to tell only what they remember. It is also okay for them to say they don't remember, if they don't. Many of those fears have been explained during the preparation and so the big worry cup is usually emptied into a small worry cup. If the counsellor sees that the child is struggling with a concept or has a real fear, she will do more work with the child. Counsellors have the contact details of the family and keep in contact with them; they often go to court to support the family, but they do not testify.

The teenage group is a group all on their own. I take my hat off to the counsellors who prepare these children. Any parent who has a teenager knows how difficult they can be; in this situation, you have a teenager with even more emotion and anger to deal with.

I mostly worked with the parent group. On a Saturday morning there can be anything up to twenty-five new parents. This figure should give an indication of how under-reported this problem is; so many other parents don't manage to get to a facility like ours because there are very few such facilities. This is why I tell parents: "Your kids are the lucky ones. They get to come here, to learn how to go about telling their story. Don't ever underestimate your support; you might not see the results now, but you will later ..."

The first-timers will all get together and sit in one room. Parents who have been to the preparation twice before don't have to sit and be taught about court procedure. However, they are encouraged to come as many times as they like before going to court, until they feel comfortable, empowered and know what to expect.

Those parents join a different group, where more family-related matters and how members are handling it, are dealt with. There is Captain Colin Morris, a dedicated policeman and personal friend, another giant in my life, who spends time with these parents and patiently explains to them exactly what happens from the time a docket is opened.

And there is the additional privilege of having on the team Agnes, a public prosecutor, who answers the legal questions posed by parents. Up to this point, the victim has been the central focus. Now the parents get the attention and help they need. They are also scared and uncertain, full of doubts and fears, and some are openly hostile.

This is a very challenging group to run. When I take roll call and ask: "What is the charge? What is the child's age? Is the perpetrator known to the child?" the parents realise that everyone in that room is in the same state of turmoil and grief. It gets very emotional sometimes. One of the most memorable mornings for me was when a black man arrived, dressed in his prison warden's outfit. There was an Afrikaans-speaking man at the other end of the room, who had been non-interactive during the entire morning. The warden stood up to tell his story, trying to maintain composure. He said, "Look at me, I wear a uniform of power, and yet my little girl was raped on the prison grounds by a prisoner who was working in the gardens." He began to cry and I felt my throat closing up. It is imperative that you allow the parents to cry and get angry. The Afrikaans man sitting on the opposite side of the room walked over to him, put out his arms and just held him. It is the one of the most powerful images I have in my mind and will never forget it.

It is also not unusual for parents to suddenly open up and tell the group that they themselves were abused. This is a huge thing for that person. This is very often the first time they have felt comfortable enough to come out and say it. Some confess out of the desperation of the situation they find themselves in. If this occurs I will inform the child's counsellor so that the parent can get some assistance in this matter, as not only is she dealing with her child's abuse, she is being catapulted back to her own past. One can only imagine the enormity of the dragon she is trying to slay.

The most excellent book I can recommend on sexual abuse victims (adult) is *The Courage to Heal*[13] by Ellen Bass and Laura Davis. I've lost count of how many copies I have bought and given to friends who have been through the slaying of that particular dragon. There is a list of recommended books in the reference section of this book. There are workshops and support groups one can attend. You need to deal with this if you haven't already. Don't give the abuser the ability to continue taking your power away from you. Don't go on living in the shadow he cast over you, which stops you from enjoying a productive life; and especially – don't allow the memory of his touch to tarnish the touch of a loved one.

---

[13] http://www.amazon.com/Courage-Heal-Revised-Expanded-Survivors/dp/0060950668

Many victims don't get beyond that boundary of secrets, which years later still causes them to sabotage their personal relationships with other adults. Take control of your life. Maybe he did, once upon a time, but this time around, you are in control.

CHAPTER 8

Keeping your child safe

What you as a parent can do

I'm willing to bet you got your sex education from your friends, not your parents! As parents, it is our total responsibility to do this, particularly in this day and age in a country where the age of consent has been dropped to sixteen for both male and female. Add to that the AIDS epidemic and unwanted teenage pregnancies, and you'll agree it must be done, just as it is your duty to strap your children into a car seat when you drive them anywhere. If you feel uncomfortable about this, tough, it's your duty to your child. Get hold of a suitable book; there are many out there, and teach your child. Don't let this opportunity be taken by someone who will distort the facts to suit their own agenda of grooming your child.

Pro-active parenting is the key. Always encourage your children to speak openly about things, no matter what the subject, and start this practice from when they're young. Do not depend on school or other people to educate your child about life. Take part in activities with your kids; show an interest in what they do. Encourage them to have other interests and to cut down time in front of a TV, on their computers and their cell phones.

Believe in your children and help them develop a healthy sense of self-esteem and self-confidence. The extra time and attention you put in is not only something you should be doing anyway as a parent, but it will be well worth the effort in terms of what you get back from your children.

Practical tips for keeping your child safe

Children who are confident and are taught about their bodies, and who know that they can talk to you about anything, no matter what, is a risk to a paedophile and not that easy to groom. Should you suspect that abuse is already happening, you will want to do what you can to create a safe space for disclosure. Intrafamilial sexual abuse is harder for the child to disclose as they live in that environment daily and have insurmountable odds to overcome.

These tips cannot guarantee your child's safety, but putting them into practise will enable your child to better protect him- or herself and increase the likelihood of them telling you if something is not right or they've gotten themselves in a difficult situation.

- From a very young age, encourage your children to speak to you; always encourage free conversation, for example, tell them about your day no matter how trivial it is, and listen to theirs. This allows them to feel comfortable engaging in conversation and to know that even small, inane events are worth talking about.

- Always talk *with* them and not *to* them, no matter if they have different views to you on certain issues. This builds confidence and tolerance of other peoples' viewpoints, and helps them to feel that their own viewpoints are allowed and respected.

- Allow yourself to show your emotions in a manner that is contained, not letting them be the parent. This encourages them to speak about their own feelings no matter how trivial they might think they are.

- Talk to your child about good and bad secrets, as secrets are part of the grooming process that the paedophile will put the child through. Use examples: good secrets are like not telling about the birthday present you bought for dad; bad secrets make your heart sad, they make you feel uncomfortable and unsafe, they keep you awake at night, they make you want to hide from people, they make you scared and worried.

- Talk to your child about appropriate and inappropriate touching. Let them know that they have a right to say NO to any type of touching that makes them feel uncomfortable or scared. Let your child know that if they are touched inappropriately, it is NEVER their fault and you will never be angry with them if they tell you about it.

- Always be actively present as a parent. Support your kids. Attend their galas, school plays and sports events. If you can't make it, find someone trustworthy who can stand in for you. Paedophiles pick out children who are not supported or supervised – this forms a starting point in the grooming process and they look out for these opportunities.

- Know where your child is at all times, as well as who they are with. If something doesn't feel right, chances are it's not right. Trust your instincts and act on them. Better to be safe than sorry.

- When your child asks to sleep over at a friend's house, make sure you get to know the parents first before agreeing to it. Go on your gut feel or, better still, have the sleepover at your place. If you don't know the parents or have not assessed their home environment, do not give in to your child's repeated demands – your child's safety is much more important than their approval of you.

- Talk openly to your kids about all aspects of the world. Tell them about paedophiles – you do not have to go into detail – simply give them enough information to help them become more aware. Let them know that these predators target children and will want them to keep a secret by offering them bribes, or through threats and fear. Let them know that they can come and tell you, no matter how hard it is for them, or how unbelievable it might sound. You will be there for them. Stand by what you say.

- Do not leave your children or teenagers unsupervised for long periods of time; with teenagers, especially, it creates an environment for the easy use of drugs and alcohol.

- If your child has a laptop or computer, make sure their time spent on it is supervised. For young children, Net Nanny programmes can be bought and downloaded to block sites not suitable for children. Teenagers who spend inordinate amounts of time on the Internet can be targets for online predators, especially teenagers going through a break up or who are difficult to speak to. They seek out other teens for affirmation of their anger or feelings, not realising that Internet predators are rife and posing as sympathetic listeners.

- Make your children memorise your contact number and address, especially small children. If they get into trouble, they – or the person from whom they are seeking help – will be able to contact you.

- Have an emergency plan. If your child is in danger or doesn't feel safe, he/she must know what to do and needs dependable people to get hold of.

- Tell your children never to accept lifts from strangers. They must also keep a safe distance from strangers' cars, even if the person seems nice.

- Have a secret password. A stranger once told a boy that something had happened and his Mum had sent him to pick him up. The boy asked the stranger for the password and used the man's confusion to run away! He and his mum had agreed on a password in case she ever had to send someone to pick him up.

- Adult strangers rarely need to ask children for help in finding things, or for directions. Adults ask adults. Let your children know this, and that if someone does stop to ask them something, they must just ignore them and walk on. Remind your children that strangers can be men *and* women.

- Tell them never to get into a car with a drunk friend – they should rather phone you, no matter what time of the night it is.
- They must never visit adults they don't know, unaccompanied.
- Enforce the 'safety in numbers' and 'buddy system' rule – never leave your buddy alone. Always walk together to and from school, the shops, or the bus stop. Never leave your buddy when you are being called aside by another adult you don't know or trust.
- Tell them to trust their feelings. If something doesn't feel right or makes them scared, they must listen to what that voice is telling them and immediately leave the place or person that makes them feel unsafe.
- They must never take short cuts that involve walking across open areas of land, back streets with abandoned buildings, isolated areas, or areas that are poorly lit. Be vigilant.
- If they are grabbed by a stranger, they must fight with all they have and make as much noise as possible. If they are able, they must bite as hard as they can. When they break free, they must keep running until they reach a safe place.

Childline encourage parents to teach their children the **Underwear Rule (PANTS)** to keep them safe from abuse. I have included this rule on its own page, overleaf, so that you can photocopy it and stick it up where both you and your child can easily see and remember it.

THE **PANTS** RULE ☞

The **PANTS** Rule

P **Privates are private**

Explain to your child that no one should ask to see or touch their private parts. Sometimes doctors, nurses or family members might have to. Explain that this is okay, but that those people should always explain why and ask if it's okay first.

A **Always remember your body belongs to you**

Let your child know that their body belongs to them, and no one else. No one has the right to make them do anything that makes them feel uncomfortable.

N **No means no**

Make sure your child understands that they have the right to say "no" to unwanted touch – even to a family member or someone they know or love.

T **Talk about secrets that upset you**

Explain the difference between 'good' and 'bad' secrets. Phrases like 'it's our little secret' are an abuser's way of making a child feel worried or scared to tell someone what is happening to them. Bad secrets make one feel sad, worried or frightened. Good secrets, like surprise parties or presents for other people, make one feel happy.

S **Speak up, someone can help**

Tell your child that if they feel sad, anxious or frightened they should talk to an adult they trust. It doesn't have to be a family member; it can also be a teacher or a friend's parent. They must keep on telling until an adult does something about it.

CHAPTER 9

The Sexual Offences Act and the Children's Act

The Sexual Offences Act

An Act has been in place for many years that compels anyone to report suspected or confirmed abuse should they come across it in whatever situation. This Act has now been amended as follows:

A: CRIMINAL LAW (SEXUAL OFFENCES AND RELATED MATTERS) AMENDMENT ACT 32 OF 2007

Chapter 7, Section 54 states that:

(1) (a) A person who has knowledge that a sexual offence has been committed against a child must report such knowledge to a SAPS official.

(b) A person who fails to report such knowledge is guilty of an offence and is liable on conviction to a fine or to imprisonment for a period not exceeding five years, or both.

2 (a) A person who has knowledge, reasonable belief or suspicion that a sexual offence has been committed against a person who is mentally disabled must report it immediately to a SAPS official.

(b) A person who fails to report it is guilty of an offence and is liable on conviction to a fine or to imprisonment for a period not exceeding five years, or both.

(c) A person who in good faith reports such a situation, shall not be liable to any civil or criminal proceedings for reporting it.

B: CHILDREN'S AMENDMENT ACT [41 of 2007]

Section 110: Reporting of abused or neglected child and child in need of care and protection.

110 (1) Any correctional official, dentist, homoeopath, immigration official, labour inspector, legal practitioner, medical practitioner, midwife, minister of religion, nurse, occupational therapist, physiotherapist, psychologist, religious leader, social service professional, social worker, speech therapist, teacher, traditional health practitioner, traditional leader or member of staff or volunteer worker at a partial care facility, drop-in centre or child and youth care centre, who on reasonable grounds, concludes that a child has been abused in a manner causing physical injury, sexual

abuse or deliberate neglect, must report that conclusion in the prescribed form (Form 25) to a designated Child Protection organisation, the Provincial Department of Social Development or a Police Official.

(2) Any person who on reasonable grounds believes that a child is in need of care and protection may report that belief to a designated Child Protection organisation, the Provincial Department of Social Development or a Police Official.

(3) The persons referred to in Section (1) or (2) must substantiate their conclusion or belief and if they make the report in good faith, they cannot be sued.

The following was taken from the manual written in 2008, which was an initiative between the Teddy Bear Clinic and the Gauteng Department of Education, compiled by Luke Lampbrecht, Anthony Wild and Tina Labuschagne.

As highlighted above, teachers are mentioned by name in the Children's Amendment Act.

- Teachers are obliged by law to report cases of abuse where they know that sexual abuse, deliberate neglect or physical injury has occurred
- Any person may report the above if they believe it has taken place
- They may report to the provincial Department of Social Development, a designated Child Protection organisation, SAPS official or Clerk of the Children's Court

- This means they can report to one or more of the above
- A designated Child Protection organisation is one that was registered by the Department of Social Development with statutory power, i.e. they can remove children – e.g. the local Child Welfare etc.
- Also, 'sexual abuse' is by definition sex with a child under sixteen years of age
- In terms of the Children's Act the cases must be reported to the local Department of Social Services as well, which implies a statutory social worker
- There are two phases to reporting: the report requiring intervention and registering of the case via a Form 25 with the Department of Social Development for the purposes of the Child Protection Register

NOTE:

Nowhere in the Sexual Offences legislation or Children's Amendment Act does it say that the offence needs to have occurred within school hours or on the school premises to make the reporting mandatory for the school and its designated officials. Please also take special note that sex between a child and a teacher/principal is not allowed. (Employment of Educators Act 76 0f 1998)

NOTE:

The new legislation requires that convicted offenders as well as suspected offenders be registered on the sex offender and child protection registers. *As a result, filling out a Form 25 is very important.*

B: PROCEDURE TO BE FOLLOWED BY THE SCHOOL IN ACUTE CASES

There are up to ten steps one must take:

1. Inform the Principal unless he/she is implicated in the abuse.

2. If the child has injuries or discloses abuse within the previous 72 hours, contact the parents immediately. This applies if it is known that the parent is not the offender or is not colluding with the offender. In cases of medical emergencies, take the child to hospital immediately. If the parents or caregivers are involved in the abuse, go to step 4. It will be the duty of the SAPS to inform the parents of what is happening, not the educator.

3. Inform the parent of the disclosure and ask whether he/she can take the child for medical attention. If the parent cannot or you cannot reach either one of them, go to step 4. If the parent is going to fetch the child, ensure that a referral letter is ready when the parent arrives to transport their child. Go to step 9.

4. Contact the nearest SAPS detective unit and ambulance service only if there is a life-threatening condition. If you do need them, ask how long you can expect to wait for them.

5. If the wait appears unacceptably long or the parents are not available, the school must take responsibility for transporting the child to the nearest appropriate

medical facility. Get permission to transport the child by ensuring that the necessary documentation providing consent for this is available on the child's record and take a copy with you to the medical centre. Inform the SAPS that you will be transporting the child and they can meet you at the medical facility.

6. Ensure that the following is brought to the hospital: Child's contact information, address and medical information. Ensure that the child's school bag is secure at the school.

7. At the hospital, the relevant information is to be handed to the medical staff. Stay with the child until the SAPS or caregivers arrive.

8. Get the relevant details and contact information of the doctor, the SAPS officer, and the social worker, where possible.

9. Once the crisis has been dealt with, the Principal should inform the IDSO[14] and the chairperson of the School Governing Body (SGB) in writing.

10. Within two days, ensure that you get the case number from the officer who assisted you. If the parent was responsible for opening the case, ensure that they have done so by asking them for the case number and confirm

---

[14] Institutional Development and Support Officer; formerly known as a school inspector

it with the relevant SAPS station. If the parent has not opened a case, inform them that you as an educator/ school have a legal duty to open a case, within ten days.

NOTE:

The Hospital may NOT turn a child away saying they need a SAPS number. The primary responsibility of the Department of Health is the well-being of the child, not the details of the criminal matter. This is a National Health instruction.

REMEMBER:

- Regardless of any agreements reached between any parties (e.g. the families agree on monetary compensation for 'damages'), the case needs to be reported to the relevant authority. Failure to do so is a criminal offence.
- Please note that reporting the case to a psychologist or social worker who does not have statutory powers is not sufficient. Statutory social workers are either employed by the State i.e. Social Development, or have statutory powers conferred by the State i.e. Child Welfare, Christelike Maatskaplike Raad (CMR), Ondersteuningsraad (OR), Suid-Afrikaanse Vroue Federasie (SAVF).

If you have had a child disclose incest, this must be reported. This is a very sensitive issue, and the child is already terrified because they have disclosed. The child must understand that other people, like the Police, will have to be involved. Telling the child is imperative so that they understand they are part of this process and not left out. The same applies if a child discloses abuse by another student under eighteen years of age at the school. The case must be reported to the South African Police Services and Department of Social Development. It is not up to the school to confront the parents; that is the job of the two bodies above. You are concerned for the child's safety. The SAPS will deal with the criminal matter, and the Department of Social services will deal with the safety of the child. If the manager of the Department of Social Development does not arrive, then contact the Senior Officer at the nearest Police Station. If still no help arrives, contact 10111 and speak to the shift supervisor.

It does not end here. You must then contact the IDSO and CESE learning curriculum and support programmes to inform them, in writing, of the steps the school has taken. Try and make very detailed notes. If you are a male teacher, it is best to have a witness with you (possibly the principal or another teacher) for your own security.

The following was taken from a manual written in 2008, which was an initiative between the Teddy Bear Clinic and the Gauteng Department of Education, compiled by Luke Lampbrecht, Anthony Wild and Tina Labuschagne.

FOR OFFENDERS UNDER THE AGE OF 16[15]:

- It is very important to know whether the sexual encounter between children over twelve and under sixteen was consensual or not. Children under twelve cannot consent and children over sixteen can. If no consent was given it is regarded as rape or sexual violation. Children aged thirteen, fourteen and fifteen who have sex, even though they consented, have still committed a crime. However, there are different ways to deal with children of different ages.

- If the victim was under twelve and/or did not consent to the sexual act, the alleged offender's parents should be informed. The process should be explained to them. (See Addendum 4).

- In terms of the new Child Justice Bill, diversion is an option that must be made available to children in conflict with the law.

- All children under eighteen can be diverted, as they are still seen as children under the Children's Act. As a result, we want to try and correct their behaviour and not use punitive methods as our first choice. However, there are conditions that they need to meet, mainly admitting to the offence, taking responsibility and trying to put the wrong right. The aim is to stop the child from offending again, and prevent others wanting to offend, as well as making the victim feel justice was done.

---

[15] Summary of Procedures for Disciplinary Hearings involving Learners (Addendum 5)

- Children over the age of fourteen, however, can face criminal prosecution.
- Children under the age of ten cannot be charged.

Between the ages of ten and fourteen, the State needs to prove that the child was criminally liable.

Relevant to (Sect.1(b)) children aged thirteen, fourteen and fifteen. The National Director of Public Prosecution (NDPP) must authorise prosecution where both role players are children.

When both are children, both must be charged.

Less than a two-year gap between children will be considered.

The school needs to contact their local Social Development office and obtain details about diversion programmes in the area as part of the criminal process – NOT as a replacement for it.

NOTE: It often happens that the police don't want to open a case when both the alleged offender and the alleged victim are children, especially when they are over twelve and under sixteen. They must open a case for investigation. If they do not, it is your responsibility to:
- Report this to the Duty Officer (Detective or Client Service Centre)
- Report it to the Station Commander
- If the Station Commander does not help, contact the provincial and national structures

The Children's Charter of South Africa[16]

Preamble

We, the delegates of the International Children's Summit held from 27 May to 1 June 1992, acting as representatives from the regions of Western Cape, Eastern Cape, Southern Cape, Northern Cape, Boland, Border, Midlands, Southern Natal, Northern Natal, Namaqualand, PWV, Eastern Transvaal, Western Transvaal, Northern Transvaal, Northern Orange Free State, Southern Orange Free State, Transkei and on behalf of all the children of South Africa.

Realising that,

all children are created equal and are entitled to basic human rights and freedoms and that all children deserve respect and special care and protection as they develop and grow and

Recognising that,

within South Africa, children have not been treated with respect and dignity, but as a direct result of *apartheid* have been subjected to discrimination, violence and racism that has destroyed families and communities and has disrupted education and social relationships and

---

[16] Source: http://www.anc.org.za/misc/childcht.html

Acknowledging that,

at the present time, children have not been placed on the agenda of any political party, or the existing government or within the Convention for a Democratic South Africa CODESA negotiations and are not given the attention that they deserve.

Taking into consideration the cultural values, languages, and traditions of all the children and,

Recognising the

urgent need for attention to improving the life of children and protecting their rights in every region, in particular those regions which have been especially subjected to violence, political unrest and poverty.

Have agreed upon the following:

Part 1

Article One

For the purposes of the Charter, a child means any person under the age of eighteen years, unless otherwise stated.

Article Two

Children have been and continue to be abused, tortured, mistreated, neglected and abandoned by the people of South Africa. Children are not treated with the respect and dignity that every human being deserves, but instead are subjected to violence, poverty, racism, and the ignorance of adults. Children continue to suffer from the inequalities of apartheid, especially in the area of education. Children do not receive proper health and medical care and attention, yet do not have the right to demand treatment. Children are arrested, tried without lawyers and held in prisons.

Children are beaten and abused by the police and by gangs and other adults. Children are the future leaders of tomorrow, but they are not given the right to participate in consultations or negotiations about their future. The government and other political parties have put children last, not first.

We therefore set forth that all children of South Africa are entitled to the following rights and protections:

Part II

Article One

1. All children have the right to protection and guarantees of all the rights of the Charter and should not be discriminated against because of his / her or his / her parents' or family's colour, race, sex, language, religion, personal or political opinion, nationality, disability or for any other reason.

2. All political parties, the government, CODESA, the future government, communities, families, and parents should do everything possible to ensure that children are not discriminated against due to his/her parents' or

family's colour, race, sex, language, religion, personal or political opinion, nationality, disability or for any other reason.

Article Two

All children have the right to a name and nationality as soon as they are born.

Article Three

1. All children have the right to express their own opinions and the right to be heard in all matters that affect his/her rights and protection and welfare.

2. All children have the right to be heard in courtrooms and hearings affecting their future rights and protection and welfare and to be treated with the special care and consideration within those courtrooms and hearings which their age and maturity demands.

3. All children have the right to free legal representation if arrested.

4. All children have the right to participate in the government of the country and special attention should be given to consultations with children on their rights and situation.

Article Four

All children have the right to freedom to practise their own religion, culture or beliefs without fear.

Article Five

Violence

1. All children have the right to be protected from all types of violence including:

    physical, emotional, verbal, psychological, sexual, State, political, gang, domestic, school, township and community, street, racial, self-destructive and all other forms of violence.

2. All children have the right to freedom from corporal punishment at school, from the police and in prisons, and at home.

3. All children have the right to be protected from neglect and abandonment.

4. All children have the right to be protected from township and political violence and to have 'safe places' and to have community centres where they can go for help and safety from violence.

5. All children have the right to be educated about child abuse and the right to form youth groups to protect them from abuse.

6. All persons have the duty to report all violence against, abuse of and neglect of any child to the appropriate authorities.

7. Children should not be used as shields or tools by the perpetrators of violence.

8. Children have the right to say no to violence.

9. The media have the duty to prevent the exploitation of children who are victims of violence and should be prohibited from the promotion of violence.

10. All children have the right to be protected from violence by the police and in prisons.

11. Children should not be obligated or forced to follow adults in their political involvements.

12. All children have the right to be free from torture, detention or any other physical or emotional violence at times of unrest or war.

13. All children have the right to be protected from drug and alcohol abuse by their parents, families and others and to be educated about these forms of violence.

14. Children have the right to a special children's Court and medical facilities to protect them from violence.

15. Special groups and organisations should be formed within the communities to protect and counsel victims of all types of violence.

16. No child should be held in prison or police cells at any time.

Article Six

Family Life

1. All children have the right to a safe, secure and nurturing family and the right to participate as a member of that family.

2. All children have the right to love and affection from their parents and family.

3. All children have the right to clothing, housing and a healthy diet.

4. All children have the right to clean water, sanitation and a clean living environment.

5. All children have the right to be protected from domestic violence.

6. All children who do not have a family should be provided with a safe and secure place to live and clothing and nutritious food within the community where they live.

Article Eight

Education

1. All children have the right to free and equal, non-racial, non-sexist and compulsory education within one department as education is a right not a privilege.

2. All children have a right to education which is in the interest of the child and to develop their talents through education, both formal and informal.

3. All teachers should be qualified and should treat children with patience, respect and dignity. All teachers should be evaluated and monitored to ensure that they are protecting the rights of the child.

4. Parents have the duty to become involved in their children's education and development and to participate in their children's education at school and at home.

5. All children have the right to play and to free and adequate sports and recreational facilities so that children can be children.

6. All children have the right to participate in the evaluation and upgrading of a curriculum which respects all the traditions, cultures and values of children in South Africa.

7. All children have the right to education on issues such as sexuality, AIDS, human rights, history and background of South Africa and family life.

8. All children have the right to adequate educational facilities and the transportation to such facilities should be provided to children in difficult or violent situations.

Article Nine

Child Labour

1. All children have the right to be protected from child labour and any other economic exploitation which endangers a child's mental, physical, or psychological

health and interferes with his/her education so that he/she can develop properly and enjoy childhood.

2. All children, especially in rural areas, should be protected from hard labour including farm, domestic or manual labour or any other type of labour.

3. All children have the right to be protected from prostitution and sexual exploitation such as pornography.

4. There should be a minimum age of employment and no child should be forced to leave school prior to the completion of matriculation for the purposes of employment.

5. There should be regulations and restrictions on the hours and types of work and penalties for those who violate these regulations.

6. All children have the right to be protected from child slavery and from the inheritance of labour or employment from their parents or family.

Article Ten

Homeless Children

1. No child should be forced to live on the streets.

2. Homeless children have the right to be protected from harassment and abuse from police, security guards and all other persons and every person has the duty to report any abuse or violence against children.

3. Homeless children have the right to a decent place to live, clothing and a healthy diet.

4. Street children have the right to special attention in education and health care.

5. Communities and families have a duty to protect their children from becoming homeless and abandoned.

6. All persons should be made aware of the plight of homeless children and should participate in programmes which act to positively eradicate the problem of homeless children.

7. The government has a duty and responsibility towards homeless children.

Resolutions

We, the children of South Africa, therefore demand that:

1. The existing government, the African National Congress, the Pan Africanist Congress, Inkatha Freedom Party, CODESA, the National Party, the Democratic Party and all other parties presently involved in negotiations acknowledge, adopt and support the Children's Charter via the establishment of committees, working groups and commissions that will ensure that children's rights will no longer be ignored in South Africa and that children will be placed first on the agenda, not last. Also, that these groups act to support existing children's structures and organisations.

2. A children's representative or council of representatives should be placed on CODESA, and within the existing and future governments. Children have the right to participate in and be consulted with about Government.

3. The future constitution and bill of rights includes special provisions for children's care and protection and development.

4. The National Children's Committee (NCC) and all other children's structures and organisations, both domestic and international, acknowledge, accept and support the Children's Charter in as many ways as possible.

5. Communities and regions act to acknowledge, adopt and support the Children's Charter and ensure that the needs of their children are addressed with urgency.

6. The delegates of the Summit act to ensure that their regions, communities, schools, families, adults and peers are informed about the Children's Charter and that there is continuing evaluation about the way forward to a culture of children's rights.

Children will no longer remain silent about their rights, but will speak and even shout out about their needs and demands.

Approved on this the 1st day of June 1992.

Resources

Important telephone numbers

Childline – 08000 55555

Netcare – 082 911

ER-24 – 084 124

Alcoholics Anonymous National Helpline – 0861 435 722

Al-Anon – 0861 25 26 66

Bobbi Bear Foundation (KwaZulu-Natal) – 072 708 0095/ 072 43 2525

Depression and Anxiety Helpline – 0800 70 80 90

Lifeline National Counselling Line – 0861 322 322

Stop Gender Violence Helpline – 0800 150 150 or 0800 428 428 or *120*7867 from any cell phone

Substance Abuse Helpline – 0800 121 314

Suicide Crisis Line – 0800 567 567

Teddy Bear Clinic (Johannesburg) – 011 484 4554

Teddy Bear Clinic (Soweto) – 011 980 8160

Teddy Bear Clinic (Krugersdorp) – 011 660 3077

TygerBear Foundation (Cape Town) – 021 931 6702 / 6717
TygerBear Foundation (24 Hour Emergency) – 082 994 4301
Vital Foundation Stop Woman Abuse Helpline – 0800 150 150

Online resources

Al-Anon for families of alcoholics – **www.alanon.org.za**
Bobbi Bear Foundation – **www.bobbibear.org.za**
Childline – **www.childlinesa.org.za**
FAMSA – family and community support services –
　　www.famsa.org.za
GRIP, counselling and support for rape survivors –
　　www.grip.org.za
Human Rights Commission – **www.sahrc.org.za**
Lawyers for Human Rights –
　　www.lhr.org.za/programme/child-rights
Lifeline – **www.lifeline.co.za**
People Opposing Women Abuse – **www.powa.co.za**
RAPCAN (Resources Aimed at the Prevention of Child
　　Abuse and Neglect) – **http://www.saferspaces.org.za**
SA National Council for Child Welfare –
　　www.childwelfaresa.org.za
SAPS Children's Corner –
　　www.saps.gov.za/child_safety
Tears Foundation, crisis intervention and counselling for
　　victims of rape and abuse (children and adults) –
　　www.tears.co.za
Teddy Bear Clinic for Abused Children – **www.ttbc.org.za**

TygerBear Foundation for Traumatised Children and
    Families – **www.tygerbear.org.za**
Volunteer Child Network, an online database of
    organisations active in reducing and preventing child
    abuse – **www.volunteerchildnetwork.org.za**

Recommended reading

- *Debbie* by Debbie Neville
- *The Filthy Lie* by Helmut Karl
- *Life beyond Your Pain* by Melanie Polatinsky
- *The Sexual Face of Violence: Rapists on Rape* by Lloyd Vogelman
- *The Best-kept Secret – Sexual Abuse of Children* by Florence Rush
- *Kids Helping Kids Break the Silence of Sexual Abuse* by Linda Foltz
- *Kids Court Support Handbook for Parents* from the Teddy Bear Clinic
- *Altar Boy – A story of life after abuse* by Andrew Madden
- *Our Fathers: The Secret Life of the Catholic Church in an Age of Scandal* by David France
- *Mothers of Incest Survivors* by Janice Tylor Johnson
- *How Long Does it Hurt? A guide to recovering from incest and sexual abuse for teenagers* by Cynthia L Mather
- *Go Ask Alice* by Beatrice Sparks

- *A Sexual Abuse Workbook for Teenage Girls* by Lulie Munson
- *Invisible Girls – The Truth about Sexual Abuse; A book for teens, young women and everyone who cares about them* by Patti Feuereisen
- The New Sexual Offences Act (www.justice.gov.za/docs/.../2008%2002%20SXOactInsert_web.pdf)

About the author

Bruna Dessena is an Advanced Life Support (A.L.S.) Paramedic who currently does shift work abroad managing remote-site clinics and attending to the emergency medical needs of all staff and families on site. While her work has taken her all over the world and exposed her to many interesting assignments and opportunities, the bulk of her career has seen her working in and around Johannesburg, known for its high crime and busy hospital casualties.

Bruna is an instructor in various aspects of emergency medicine and continues to teach when back home in Cape Town, where she now resides. She maintains her 'on-the-road' emergency skills by volunteering her services to a community-based and sponsored medical emergency service in Hout Bay, and by doing stand-in shifts for various emergency services companies in and around Cape Town and Johannesburg. In 2015, she completed her Masters degree in Emergency Medicine, with her thesis focusing on child abuse disclosure during medical treatment.

Bruna was a volunteer counsellor for both Childline and the Teddy Bear Clinic. At the latter, she was also a trainer and Senior Facilitator preparing children and parents for court. She currently presents lectures on child abuse to paramedics and doctors, as well as med-school, nursing and social work students at various universities, colleges and hospitals in the Western Cape and Johannesburg. Bruna also does talks for teachers and parents at schools in and around the Western Cape.

Bruna has two children, Themba and Khangiswe. She has published a second book, *Tales from my Stethoscope*, featuring fascinating real-life stories of her life on the road as a paramedic, told with a dash of her quirky humour.

Other titles by Bruna Dessena:

Tales from my Stethoscope

True stories of life on the streets from a not-too-serious South African paramedic

Bruna takes you behind the scenes of accidents, sudden illness, shootings and human revelry gone wrong. You'll experience the fun and excitement of Johannesburg on a Saturday night … but you'll also go to the lonely places where old people suffer in silence and children aren't properly cared for; where rich people die alone, violence is fueled by alcohol, and calls start with "I didn't think it would happen to me …".

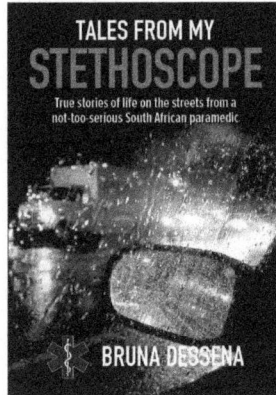

You'll read about running a clinic on a mine in deepest Africa and being the resident paramedic on a geo-survey ship plying the waters around the globe. You'll fly helicopters over cities praying that the patient survives, and you'll be there in the middle of farming country helping to amputate a leg caught in a harvester.

If you can stomach the drama and the quirky humour used to get through harrowing situations, you'll get to the end of these fascinating tales with a deeper understanding of the human condition and renewed admiration and gratitude for those who listen and act when we call out in distress.

Available from:
www.publisher.co.za
Amazon, iBookstore, B&N

Be proactive about your child's safety!

BOOK A <u>FREE</u>* CHILD ABUSE TALK

AT YOUR

SCHOOL
WORKPLACE
INSTITUTION
UNIVERSITY OR COLLEGE
POLICE STATION
HOSPITAL OR CLINIC

For bookings, email:
brunadessena@hotmail.com

*<u>All talks are offered free of charge</u>.
Travel and accommodation costs for talks outside the
Western Cape are for the organiser's account.